Showering with the Alligators

*How a Jewish Princess Became
Trailer Trash*

Alexa Rossy

Copyright © 2023 by Alexa Rossy

Table of Contents

Dedication 7
Introduction 9
Bingo and Yellow Roses The Test! Outdoor RV Resorts,
Everglades City, Florida, 2002 10
2002 19
    May 2002 I Never Thought I Would Be . . . "Showering with the Alligators" Or . . . "How a Jewish Princess Became Trailer Trash" 20
    Departure and First Week
    Trailer Trash Goes From Mobile to Memphis June 2002 25
    Greetings from Graceland! May 2002 27
    Settle Back. This Is a Long One. 2002 30
    Kincaid and Francesca Revisited 33
    Wild Horses and Desperados 36
    Golddiggers and Close Encounters 39
    Red Wigglers, Ghosts, and Moose Drool June 2002 43
    Earth, Wind, and Snow . . . Where's the Beach? 2002 47
    Cody, Wyoming Summer 2002
    Bubbling, Gushing, and Swan Lake 50
    Dust Devils, Switchbacks, and Mormons
    June 2002 On the Road to Moab, Utah 54
    Hoodoos, Smokey the Bear, and Totem Poles 58
    "Like a Virgin*" in the Dicey Desert July 2002 62
    Whale-Watching, Wine Tasting, and Brothels 66
    Trona, Death Valley, and Flip-Flops July 2002 69
    The North Rim, Route 66, and UFOs June – July 4, 2002 72
    The Roswell Incident Roswell, New Mexico 75
    Bats, Water and Trees July 2002 78
    August 2002 70 Days on the Road. The Conclusion 80
    Things hardly ever seen or heard on the road: 85
2003 89
    Groundhogs to Blame for Landslide 90
    Clouds on the Lawn and Study in Contrasts 94
    Time to Say Goodbye . . . to North Carolina 97
    Just Passin' Through Tennessee, "The Volunteer State" 99
    Sunflowers, Chuck Berry, and the Longest Day (Not the Movie) 102

The Color Green, Roadkill, and Altitude Sickness 107
San Juan Skyway: Aspen to Ouray to Telluride to Durango
to Silverton Or "The Loop," Part 1 110
Riding the Rail – Durango/Silverton Friday, June 27 113
Celebrity Sightings, Silly Names, and Characters 116
"Wide"oming, The Cowboy State, the Oregon Trail,
and More Mormons June 30 – July 2 119
Bathless and Battlegrounds 123
2002 (or so), July 4th,
Red Lodge, Montana Sparkle, Pop, Fizzle, Whinny 125
Lewis and Clark Found This Place, and So Did We!
Great Falls, MT 128
Gurgle, Drip, Freeze . . . Glacier National Park,
and Going-to-the-Sun Road, 2003 St. Mary, Montana 131
Powwows and Snow Cones 134
Coeur d'Alene, Seaplanes, and the 14th Hole 2003 137
Moose Drool and Music 140
Smoke Jumpers 142
Trivia From the Road 145
Sun Valley — "Roses and Lollipops" 148
Idaho, the Schlep State 151
Eugene, Oregon . . . Worth the Drive 2003 153
And a River Runs Through It—
The Northwest Passage Sunday, July 27 157
Who is Bob Witson? Deer Lodge, MT July 2003 160
Vroom, Vroom, Vroom August 1–6, Bike Week
Sturgis, South Dakota 164
Love Affairs, and What I Learned on the Road 168

2004 173
The Passenger Seat 174
Sunday, Father's Day Kitschy Kitschy Coo 176
The Burning Bush Saturday, June 26, 2004 178
Local Lingo in North Carolina 180
Estonian Husband Won't Tell Wife to Get Off His Back
July 8, 2004 182

July 22, 2004 Go Cat, Go..184
July 20, 2004 The Roads Most Traveled..186
Kentucky Woman July 25, 2004..188
July 28, 2004 MapQuest..191
Shaggy Dog Story — Maybe . . . July 29, 2004..................................194
The Mormon Conquest July 30, 2004...196
Utah — Eau de Saline July 31, 2004..199
Forgotten Tidbits August 1, 2004..201
Drilling-Blasting-Hauling-Crushing..203
One Step up from the Manger August 4, 2004..................................205
2005...207
She's Gone Again! June 11, 2005...208
"Rainy Night in Georgia" June 18, 2005..210
Beauty and the Born-Agains June 16, 2005.......................................213
"Mack the Knife" and the Outer Banks June 22, 2005......................216
Pitch, Yaw, and Roll Or How 12 Seconds Changed the World..........219
Swashbucklers and Shipwrecks The Outer Banks..............................222
October 12, 2005 Serendipity and Ethel..225
Memory Lane. Or, What Lasts Forever?..229
2006...233
June 2006 "Tin-Can Living Becomes Fashionable".........................234
July 2006 Fireflies Lighting Up the Night...237
T-Rex Goes to Dollywood July 20, 2006...240
October 3, 2006 Can You Keep a Secret?..244
Drag Queens in Tennessee August 12, 2006......................................248
2007...253
Put Your Dreams in Motion! (Whatever They Are) July 2007..........254
Run Bunny, Run, Burnsville, NC July 2007......................................256
My Old Kentucky Home..259
T-Rex in Tulsa July 2007..261
The Breakfast Club July 2007..264
Lamar, CO. August 2007...268
Just Ducky in Aspen August 2007...271
Taking the Plunge, Glenwood Springs, CO August 2007.................274
Vortex-Schmortex, Sedona, Arizona August 2007............................278

2008 283
    June 14, 2008 Suddenly this Summer!..284
    July 26, 2008 Shock and Awe..286
2009 291
    September 12, 2009 Whatcha Doin'?..292
    April 23, 2009 Rhapsody in Blue..295
    Have Pungi, Will Travel June 2, 2011...300
    Roll Me Over, and Do It Again July 2009...303
    Frolicking with the Oldies December 30, 2009.................................306
2011 311
    Rusty and Edna June 13, 2011...312
2015 317
    The Ark Encounter (as in Noah's), October 2018..............................318
2016 323
    Sometimes the Getaways Get You!
    January 2016, Coldest Weekend of the Year in Florida......................324
    June 21, 2016 Roan Mountain, North Carolina "Think Pink"..........329
2017 335
    June 18, 2017 So, You Think You Can Go RVing?...........................336
    June 19, 2017 Pastels, Pickets (Fences), and Porches........................338
    June 22, 2017 Old Man River..340
    July 1, 2017 Deer Catchers and Koozies...342
    June 26, 2017 Meanwhile, Back at the Ranch 345
    July 2, 2017 Roswell, New Mexico
    "The Truth Is Out There . . ." Maybe..348
Acknowledgments..353
About the Author..355

Dedication

For my unexpected muse, Craig, aka T-Rex.
Without him, there would be no book.

Introduction

Trailer Trash Chronicles are my stories, written as emails from the road. They describe fifteen years of traveling around the United States of America in an RV. Oy vey! The recipients were my friends and family, who I fondly refer to as my "trashettes."

In the beginning, I was a fifty-seven-year-old widow. I was in unchartered territory, a reluctant road worrier—not *warrior*—and my Jewish princess upbringing on Miami Beach did not lend itself to tin-can living. But, with the persuasion of an attractive alpha male, and my need for a new chapter in my life, I was able to leave my zip code and stilettos behind. It's called taking a risk.

The stories are placed more or less in chronological order by year, but each story stands alone (much like the cheese). Some names have been changed, but the places and factoids are all for real.

All of what you will read comes from my memories, observations, sense of humor and sometimes irreverent take on things.

Thank you for turning the pages or swiping to the next. I promise you a laugh, some history and geography lessons and maybe even a teardrop or two.

Let's get going, and keep it going, just as I have learned to do.

Bingo and Yellow Roses
The Test!
Outdoor RV Resorts, Everglades City, Florida, 2002

This was to be the "sneak preview" of longer trips, if I survived the weekend. Going to Everglades City for the nightlife is like going to the moon for a suntan. It was the end of another Miami madness week, and I needed a brain break. Everglades City is about as small town as one can get to in the state of Florida and still only drive two hours from Miami. I could hardly wait to get on the road.

Craig, the fun-loving alpha male, is the man who introduced me to RVing. I nicknamed him T-Rex because he does have some prehistoric traits. He is a fearless, muscular 6'3". He will go anywhere (except the ballet), eat anything, sleep anywhere, and though he can be very dear, he occasionally roars. T-Rex owns a 34-foot Airstream trailer that sits on a concrete slab in the backyard of his house. It makes it very convenient for last-minute getaways. The tin can on wheels will end up becoming our favorite mode of travel, but in this instance, it's our escape and a test to see if a Jewish princess can adapt. Quickly as you can say "Trailer

Trash," we hooked up the Airstream to Craig's Dodge diesel truck and readied ourselves for departure.

The Airstream has a fully equipped kitchen and bathroom, and is already stocked with the essential kitchen tools and bath toiletries. There is not too much I need to think about when packing except what food and clothes to bring along. So, off we went with the mindset of disconnecting from all the big-city buzz and trappings to relax and recharge our human batteries.

We arrived at the Outdoor RV Resorts Park at 7:30 p.m. It was Friday night, and there wasn't a Starbucks or AMC movie theater in sight. There is absolutely nothing going on. Even the alligators are resting. How wonderful! Nevertheless, we arrived after sunset, and it was time to experience the RV park social life—whatever that was—after dark.

Typically, on trips, we like to go out and explore in a new area, but most RVers, no matter the location of the park, usually spend their time doing the same basic things. They putter around, gardening, grilling, fishing, walking their dogs, and washing their trailers. Competitive resting outside on lounge chairs is another main activity.

But what do they do at night in a little town with no movie theater, no restaurants, and not even a shopping mall?

Well, according to the flamingo-pink, hand-painted sign posted at the park entrance, that night, and every Friday night is bingo. As soon as we saw that sign, T-Rex and I exchanged knowing glances. Of course we would be playing bingo.

We prepared ourselves for the bingo adventure by spraying on a half gallon of Cutter's mosquito repellent, putting on our sandals, and walking to the recreation hall. It was only a five-minute walk, but we passed several spaces where other RVs were parked. It was fun to see the different ways people embellished their metal mansions.

Some had miniature picket fences, some had colorful party lights strung across the awnings, and yes, some had plastic pink flamingos guarding their front doors, just like we do.

Because of its location, Everglades City is very quiet. It's surrounded by the Barron River and Chokoloskee Bay. There are only one or two roads in the whole town. There are no high-rise buildings and no chain stores (actually, no stores at all unless you count the bait shop). The big-city noises of expressway traffic, sirens blasting, and crowds in the streets are nonexistent.

As we approached the two-story screened building, the only sounds we could hear in the unfamiliar but welcome silence of night were the high-pitched hums of mosquitos planning their next assault and a woman's voice calling out "B-Six. I-Four . . ."

We walked into a brightly lit room full of what looked like Walmart shoppers, most retired and overweight, and many with eight bingo cards in front of them.

Based on a quick observation, I was pretty sure I was among the youngest, slimmest, and still-working people in the group. No problem, but I couldn't help wondering . . . Was I looking into my future? And if I was, why wasn't the crystal ball Swarovski?

Some of our fellow players had brought special bingo lights to aim at their cards. Others had small flower arrangements for their tables and little cases that held bingo accessories. With all this accoutrement just for bingo, I wondered how they ever traveled cross-country in a 400-square-foot box with wheels.

But back to bingo. I now call it "big bingo" because it was professionally done. There was a large electronic board recording the caller's numbers. The winners were verified for accuracy by "checkers" who patrolled the tables (some in wheelchairs). The cashier paid out as much as $30.00 for a winning card. To get into the game, we bought one card each for $2.00. We looked around for a place to sit and were waved over to a table right up front. Helen was sitting there all alone, except for her six cards and her little accessory case. She said the table was usually full but that all the regulars hadn't come that night. Helen looked about seventy-five years old, but she quickly told me she was one of the oldest people in the park, so I recalculated her at eighty-five.

There are a lot of RV parks where travelers come in and rent a space just for a night or two. This park has spaces that people own and can rent out when they aren't using them. Most of the people there tonight were owners and therefore "regulars." In Florida, we call them "snowbirds," and they stay for about six months during the winter. Because of that, almost everyone in the park knows everyone else, but no one knew us. We could feel the stares from the back of the room. T-Rex and I were a novelty that night, and even in our sandals and walking shorts, about as far from the regulars as you can get. Maybe it was my dangling gold hoop earrings, or more likely, T-Rex's big muscles.

Most of my bingo skills had been forgotten long ago, after

my mother's 85th birthday party. I did remember that one solid line going any which way on the card was a win. But I soon discovered that there were also Xs, borders, corners, and full-card configurations to be played.

Helen suggested that we buy additional cards to make it "more exciting." She seemed to be a pro, so we took her advice and sprang for two more cards.

In the course of fourteen games, there was an ice cream break (two scoops for $1.00, and the toppings are free), and Helen and I chatted. She and her husband had been married for sixty-five years and had been coming to that same park since 1983. He died five years before, and she'd said, "It's been very hard without him. He was a perfect man, and everyone in the park just loved him." Helen had children, grandchildren, and a place in the Midwest, where she lived from May through November. In this park, she owned her own space, her fifth-wheel trailer, a small fishing boat, and her memories. As if she were going for a manicure, Helen casually told me she was having angioplasty the following Wednesday in Naples, FL, thirty miles away.

She lived in space #65 and invited us to visit. I told her we'd come by the next day. The games were over at 9:00 p.m., and we didn't win, but we came close, which was fun.

The next day, T-Rex and I rode our bicycles over to space #65. Helen was puttering inside and invited us right in. Her face was flushed from cleaning out her refrigerator, and with relief rather than grace, she plopped into her brown leather Archie Bunker recliner. I made note of her blue eyes and her white hair, which was probably never colored.

The first thing she showed us was a picture of herself with her husband. She and "the perfect man" were standing in front of their commercial plant and flower nursery greenhouse. She was at least 75 pounds slimmer in the picture, and as if reading my mind, she told me that "The minute I stopped working, I gained weight."

I learned that the Mitchells had provided plants and flowers for every important party, wedding, and bar mitzvah around Illinois, near Chicago's farmlands. They ran the business together. They had fifty delivery trucks, which Helen drove (not all at once), and two hundred employees. In her spare time, Helen was an EMT on an ambulance. Had the light suddenly changed, or was I starting to see Helen in a different one? It's the old, old lesson: "You can't judge a book by its cover." And this no-nonsense, church-going cover contained hundreds of pages of accomplishments, people, and places.

Speaking of books, Helen's daughter, Ann, had written a bestselling book about coffee cakes. She had submitted it to the Miami book fair for the next year, which is a really big deal. As soon as I saw the book full of recipes and colored photos of delicious-looking cakes, I knew "The Cake Lady" would be one of my girlfriend's birthday presents that year. We finally said goodbye after admiring her RV and some beautiful yellow roses she had on the end table. She'd said, "Oh, I grow them in the little yard here." It was a nice visit, and I wondered who would be taking Helen to Naples for her procedure. She never mentioned it.

At 8:30 the next morning, after getting out of the

Airstream's less-than-ample shower, I walked into the cozy living area and noticed something inside the doorway that hadn't been there earlier. There was a tiny crystal bud vase holding two perfect yellow roses, and beside it, two copies of *The Cake Lady* book. There was no note, and none was needed—just an unspoken connection. I knew that Helen had enjoyed our visit as much as we had. My eyes welled up, and my heart did, too. I was truly touched by this sweet and totally unexpected gesture from someone who, twelve hours before, had been a total stranger. It turns out to be one of the great things about traveling in an RV. There are special moments to be had, all kinds of people to meet, and the time to get to know them.

As I puttered around that afternoon, I pondered . . . why aren't there more of these kinds of moments at home? Why, with so many wonderful friends, was I often too busy to visit with them? Instead, why are we all constantly leaving voicemails and emails for each other? Why can't we take the time and smell the roses like the ones Helen left me?

In our attempts to feel connected and be connected, are we isolating ourselves even more? Are we letting our busy lives get in the way of genuine human contact? It was certainly something to think about, and I continued to do so. On the two-hour ride back I thought about it more and more. Just as the Miami skyline came into view, I came up with the answer.

After my touching experience with bingo and yellow roses, I knew what works for me to feel connected. It's simple. All it takes is a one-on-one conversation with someone like Helen. It takes realizing that bingo night is really an old-fashioned version of happy hour, and that sometimes big bingo is all the nightlife I need. And finally, for me, sometimes it takes going all the way to the edge of the Everglades to get back to center. The sneak preview TEST earned me an A+.

I was ready for the road and happy to become Trailer Trash because Trailer Trash, for me, means discovering interesting people, the places they travel, and the lives they have led.

Love to you all.
Alexa
Aka Trailer Trash

2002

May 2002
I Never Thought I Would Be . . .
"Showering with the Alligators"
Or . . . "How a Jewish Princess Became
Trailer Trash"

My childhood was nearly perfect, growing up with a loving family, lots of friends, and the glamour of Miami Beach in the 1950s. The hotels, sports cars, and nightclubs were as common as coconut palms, and most of us beach kids felt privileged just being born in the right place at the right time.

My pampered path to adulthood included a college degree, a marriage, the birth of my son, and a divorce. The silver spoon was slowly tarnishing as life's bumps started to get in the way.

The next marriage brought bliss along with sadness. When my second husband died of kidney cancer, I thought the charmed life that I had led was finally and forever over. I was just fifty years old, and I was a widow.

Recovering from loss is an individual process. In my case, distractions of the risk-taking kind worked best to keep me going. I accepted all invitations for activities outside my comfort zone. After all, hadn't I just learned that life can be short and not necessarily sweet? Adventure became a best friend, and the more spontaneous, the better. So perhaps it was not all that surprising that when a man I barely knew asked me to join him one afternoon on his motorcycle, I said yes without hesitation. The man "I barely knew" was Craig, later to be nicknamed T-Rex. He had been a customer (of my late husband's) of our boat trailer business. He was a career captain on commercial airlines for twenty-seven years and was now flying private jets for a big company in Miami. When he wasn't flying, he was racing offshore powerboats and riding motorcycles. He was sixty-four years old, 6'3", a gym rat, a confirmed bachelor, not Jewish, and very attractive.

I quickly calculated that if this alpha male could safely fly DC-9s with two hundred passengers aboard, then I would probably be all right on the back of his motorcycle. I accepted his offer.

The afternoon turned into evening. The evening turned into other afternoons and evenings. The motorcycle rides turned into day trips, and the day trips turned into weekends. In between bike rides, we flew in small planes and drove in fast cars. My pilot friend and I were on a nonstop course of adventure. The roads and the skies were my gloom chasers, and I was learning to love life again.

And then, one day came the riskiest offer yet. The pilot said, "I'm going to buy an RV, and I want you to travel with me in it." Now I was out of my comfort zone. Riding on the back of a bike was one thing, but trailers were not something that anyone I knew had, or ever, God forbid, wanted to have. *Glamping* was not a word that had been created yet. Would this be an adventure or a nightmare? How would I possibly manage in such a small space? Without walk-in closets? No bubble baths? No privacy? And being far away from everything familiar for long stretches?

I didn't commit immediately, but I did tag along with him to look at several different RV models. He decided on a 28' Airstream trailer. It would be pulled with his diesel truck. His motorcycle would go up into the truck bed via a ramp. We would bring bicycles, too. I was starting to picture a modern version of "The Grapes of Wrath," and I still wasn't sure if I could or would fit into that picture. However, the shiny little trailer had a certain retro charm, and I was warming up to the idea.

Yes, I finally decided that I could try this, and so after much ado about everything, we left Miami on a short test run to Everglades City.

Now for the rest of the stories . . .

My first time in an RV park (and they say you always remember your first time) was spent in Starke, Florida, at a KOA, which stands for Kamp Grounds of America. Who knew? I was totally clueless. What I did know was that Starke's claim to fame is the prison that houses "Old Sparky," the electric chair. I hoped this was not a bad omen, but I didn't think it could possibly be a good one. Cooking in the teensy galley was challenging, but nothing compared to showering in a trailer bathroom where there is barely room for the soap.

"No problem," said the pilot. "The park has public showers. All you have to do is walk down to that green building near the water."

I headed for the building on newly pedicured feet, with my soap-on-a-rope, towel, and hair dryer in hand, and there they were . . . prehistoric looking in all their glory, sunning themselves on the rocks: alligators of every size. The heat of the day suddenly gave me chills as I walked past them, hoping my hot-pink Crocs would make me less of a target—sort of one of the family. They did not move, they did not seem to notice me, and before you think that I was senselessly brave, I will tell you that there was a chain-link fence that separated them from the path I was on. Nevertheless, "Showering with the alligators" became the phrase I used from then on to indicate a scary or unique experience on the road. And there were many.

I never thought I would enjoy RVing as much as I do. It turns out that it's more relaxing than most vacations. You can stop anytime, linger, explore, or move on at will. Your house is with you all the time. You don't have to pack and unpack, and of course, the bathroom is always close by—not to mention the wildlife. I've been a boot's length away from buffalos in Yellowstone National Park and a boat length away from whales off the California coast.

After a few more trips during which I didn't break or burn anything and actually proved to be quite resourceful, the pilot decided we should get something with a few more creature comforts. We now travel pulling a 36-foot fifth wheel with an ample shower and 40-inch flat-screen TV. It's hardly roughing it anymore, although sometimes I do miss the little Airstream. This princess made sure that the new king-size bed is made with 500+ thread count sheets, and the sterling silver Grande Baroque flatware just might accompany us on our next journey.

I'm grateful for those first-time experiences. They taught me to push my personal envelope and to fully engage in a lifestyle completely out of my zip code and my upbringing. With a few exceptions, most of my friends were totally aghast at my travel arrangements and the whole trailer thing, but after a few "happy hour" visits and movie nights in the trailer when we were back home, the girlfriends have all become trailer park princesses. They leave their stilettos and sneakers at the door, as well as the outside world, for just a few hours. Nobody knows we're inside, and we don't care. They understand that after every trip (that I never thought I would take), I return with my sense of humor intact (but not necessarily my nails), and lots of stories that we all share. I've learned that when life gets in the way, the detours often provide unexpected pleasures and opportunities to recapture yourself in different ways than you ever thought possible.

In the beginning, my emails, "Trailer Trash Chronicles," were written out of my insecurities. They were a way of staying connected to the lifestyle I was leaving behind. They comforted me at the end of the day like a conversation with a good friend. And of course, they helped me remember all the places and feelings I was experiencing. They are stories about unusual people and their occupations. They are stories about the magnificence of the natural beauty in the United States, and they are stories about the psychological/emotional challenges faced by a gently bred woman traveling in a tin can with an alpha male. I have trailered myself into a freedom junkie and an observer of human nature. The addiction continues. And every once in a while, when no one is looking, I dust off my rhinestone tiara, count my blessings, and think about where I'd like to go next time.

Departure and First Week
Trailer Trash Goes From Mobile to Memphis
June 2002

We left Miami in the shiny silver 28-foot Airstream trailer. Since I didn't know exactly where we were going, or what or whom we might encounter, it was impossible to pack. Plus, the closet in the Airstream is the size of a phone booth. Craig was being remarkably patient and reminded me that in America, there are stores in case I forgot something. He immediately ruined that by reminding me in his superior captain's tone of voice that he had been able to get ready in a half hour and only took a small suitcase. Good for him. More room for my stuff.

I'm feeling very relaxed, finally. Part of the reason is that Southerners are restful in their ways, we are in the Deep South, and the restfulness is contagious.

But here's a revelation as to the real reason why: Most vacations are defined by a beginning and an end, with the vacation activities pre-planned. There are reservations to keep, a hit list of must-see attractions, and there's no leeway for variations. In our case, south, north, east, west . . . anything goes! It's a very sketchy itinerary with the ability to stop, linger, explore, or take a pass on a daily, even hourly basis. It's a freedom I haven't experienced before on vacation, and I guess I'm a freedom junkie. Every job I've ever had allowed me a flexible schedule. "Nine to Five" might have worked for Dolly, and I understand that non-scheduling isn't for everyone, but it sure works for me. I haven't nibbled a cuticle since we left.

Also, this Airstream trailer is far from "roughing it." We're not camping out (I'm not that good a sport), but rather enjoying all the basic creature comforts: AC, gas range (I do like my own cooking), bathroom, stereo (classical music station playing now). So maybe it's not normal for most travelers. It's certainly not conventional, but the options are limitless, as are the towns, the people, the foods, the music, the weather, and the unexpected. I'm not exactly sure where we stored everything or how all the mechanical systems work yet, but I haven't broken anything, and I've discovered that I'm quite resourceful. Now, if only I could remember where I stashed the Hershey's Kisses and get Craig to stop watching *Hawaii Five-O*. I'll be in touch after the first stop. I'm looking forward to your messages. Thank you for all of them.

Much love,

Alexa
Aka Trailer Trash

Greetings from Graceland!
May 2002

Elvis may have left the building, but in Memphis, he is still everywhere. We are staying in the Memphis RV Park on Elvis Presley Blvd. The Heartbreak Hotel is right next door for people who travel the normal way and stay in rooms that don't move every two or three days.

Questions: Did I want to marry Elvis when I was fourteen? Yes, I did. Did I want to cook and clean for him? Yes, I did. Did I dance to all of his hits on *Tens Bandstand* in Miami? Yes, I did. God, this is tacky.

Anyway, first we stopped in Tupelo, MS, and visited the birthplace of Elvis. It was a one-room house that cost his father $180.00. Did you know that Elvis had a twin brother who was stillborn? (You may need to know this on *Jeopardy*, on a crossword puzzle, or Trivial Pursuit someday.) And while I'm at it, did you know that Elvis's manager, Colonel Parker, was such a scam artist that he painted sparrows yellow and sold them as canaries? And just two more things. Did you know that next to the White House, more people visit Graceland than any other house in the USA? And did you know who Elvis called every day of his life? His mother. My kinda guy!

We ambled from Mobile to Memphis, stopping wherever anything looked interesting. It was mostly rural, one-stoplight towns, no movies, no strip centers—just rolled hay and cows. I'm discovering that I like all that, and we found a wonderful spot for lunch right next to a lock and dam with warm breezes and rushing waters.

It's not the News Cafe on South Beach by any stretch, but just as fun for now.

It's only been a week, but I've really tried to eat and cook healthy things. However, today I fell from grace near Graceland, snacking on Hostess Twinkies and Little Debbie Oatmeal Crème Pies.

Please go to the gym for me because it's not lookin' too good for future meals. However, I feel great—always busy with guidebooks and RV directories and writing to you all. There is a lot to remember and plan with the trailer and absolutely nothing that I learned in college.

We spent five hours in Graceland, and now I love Elvis even more. In spite of the wall-to-wall shag carpeting, what started out as a tacky tourist event turned into an unbelievable tour of his home and an in-depth look at his life, achievements, and personality. It turns out he was a very decent man and a very charitable one. We saw hundreds of thank-you plaques hanging on the walls in one of Graceland's huge rooms.

That being said, I turned down the offer to stay a night in the "Hunk a Hunk of Burnin' Love" suite in the Heartbreak Hotel. I think I'm finally Elvis-ed out.

Tomorrow, we head for the Ozarks, through Arkansas, and onto Branson, MO, where it's cold and 45 to 75 degrees. We have spoken with many of the locals, and I've been called "ma'am" and "little lady" over a dozen times. What can I say? It's another world. More in a few days.

Much love on the 12th day.

Alexa
Aka Trailer Trash

Settle Back. This Is a Long One.
2002

What we know about Arkansas . . . It's where Hernando de Soto looked for the Fountain of Youth, Jesse James held up stagecoaches, and saloon crusher Carrie Nation buried her hatchet. Hard to believe that Slick Willie, aka Bill Clinton, is from here as well. This is a place that is painfully quaint, plus there is a simple quality of life that is fast disappearing in other areas.

It's also the birthplace of General Douglas MacArthur and the state where Walmart's Sam Walton started his tour de force against Kmart in Bentonville. On the downside, this state makes me remember Governor Orval Faubus. It was he who called in the National Guard to keep nine black students from attending Little Rock's central high school in 1957.

Missouri, on the other hand, contributed Harry Truman, the Pony Express, JC Penney, Mark Twain, kewpie dolls, the strongest earthquake in the lower forty-eight states, and the world's tallest woman at 8'4".

Also, Walt Disney spent his boyhood in Marceline, MO, and modeled Disneyland's Main Street USA after it. Lucky for the world, he didn't grow up in Newark! If that were the case, Mickey Mouse would have been nothing more than a rodent. All this, and not a place for miles to get a good manicure.

Also, according to this week's *USA Today*, Arkansas is the obesity capital of the USA, with over fifty percent of the population too heavy for their own good health. This is probably because every three feet there is a restaurant serving biscuits and white gravy (looks like Elmer's Glue), smoked ham, and fruit cobblers. Finding a piece of fresh cantaloupe here was almost as exciting as my first kiss.

And then there is Branson, the little Las Vegas of Middle America. Branson is the second most visited tourist town in the US after Orlando. It has over thirty-five musical theaters (this could become my new happy place), *and* the strip of theaters in the new section of town looks like a mini Las Vegas.

So far, we have seen shows starring Andy Williams, Glen Campbell, and someone named Shoji Tabuchi. He does with a violin what Victor Borge did with a piano, plus a cast of thousands. Andy Williams at 75 years old is full-voiced and spry. He has built his own "Moon River" theater, which is first class and would rival anything we have in Miami. Tickets are a reasonable $20.00 to $30.00. Do you remember the Glen Campbell show from 1969? It's the same year my son Jeremy was born and when the first astronaut went to the moon. Campbell surprised our audience with an unexpected appearance and sang many of his hits. Thirty years later, he still plays a spirited guitar and sings like honey-coated grits. The memories came flooding back: "Gentle on my Mind," "Galveston," "Wichita Lineman."

It's showtime again, so I'm signing off. Love to you all, and thanks for your messages.

Alexa
Aka Trailer Trash

Kincaid and Francesca Revisited

My son said, "Mom, Iowa is supposed to be the worst state to travel across," and so I expected to be bored by a flat and uninspired landscape that borders America's breadbasket (with not a bagel in sight, by the way). Was I ever surprised! Iowa is not flat. There are rolling hillsides with picturesque farmlands, clapboard houses, town squares, Amish farmsteads, and then the great serendipity . . . the bridges of Madison County, from the book and movie of the same name in the small town of Winterset, Iowa. There are six covered bridges that people from all over the world travel to see. Why were the bridges covered? Two reasons: to protect the building materials, and so horses would cross them more readily thinking they were going into the barn. I stood on Roseman Bridge, where the book's character (Clint Eastwood in the film), Robert Kincaid, went to take photographs for *National Geographic*. Then I went to Francesca's (Meryl Streep's) farmhouse and stood at the window where she saw Kincaid washing up at the pump. The house is still fully propped as in the movie, and the old green pickup truck that was so well described in the book is parked outside. The aura of their love affair still lingers, and just for a moment, I was part of that story. For your information, Robert Waller, the author, has written an epilogue to *Bridges*. It is titled "A Thousand Country Roads." I purchased it on the spot but have not had time to read it all.

The town of Winterset is also famous because it is John Wayne's birthplace, and so we went to see the house where he was born. Coincidentally, that day would have been his 95th birthday, and so the tour was free. Happy birthday, Duke! His house was bigger than Elvis's.

We have been blessed with beautiful weather, and there is no humidity, so I have very straight hair, and that alone is a good reason to keep traveling. Today is the start of week three, and we have traveled through Iowa into South Dakota. I'm glad I didn't have to do this in a covered wagon. No wonder so many of the women went mad or died young.

The West has a blindsiding effect when you arrive at the Missouri River. The terrain change is almost disorienting. Imagine the Lewis and Clark Expedition, traveling through these waters in their search for a waterway to the Pacific. They were paid $2,500.00 for their 8,000-mile, 862-day journey and spent almost one third of their time traversing the Dakotas. It's the original long haul!

While you girls (and some of my guy friends, as well) have been sipping wine and munching niçoise salad, I had my first buffalo burger, accompanied by a real sarsaparilla, and am within striking distance of Mt. Rushmore. I'm sure I will have more to report because we're staying in Deadwood, South Dakota, for at least five days and will be on the motorcycle every day taking side trips. Remember that this is the state where Teddy Roosevelt shot a buffalo (there is no Bambi syndrome out West), Peggy Lee learned to sing, and Lawrence Welk learned to talk (he spoke only German until he was twenty-one). Cream of Wheat was invented here. Angie Dickinson was born here. Wild Bill Hickock was gunned down here, and Kevin Costner danced with wolves here.

That's all for now. The open road is waiting. Love to you all. I hope I'm not boring you with my email reports, but it's a great way for me to record my adventures.

XXs,

Alexa
Aka Trailer Trash

P.S. Remember, if you have to squat, take your spurs off.

Wild Horses and Desperados

While touring the West in 1935, Frank Lloyd Wright exclaimed, "I've been about the world a lot and pretty much over our own country, but I was totally unprepared for the Dakota Badlands, an endless supernatural world more spiritual than earth but created out of it." So, hello from Deadwood, South Dakota. This girl from Miami Beach was a lot less prepared than the famous architect, but here goes . . . I am totally overwhelmed by the "Vest Pocket of the Rockies." It was deemed a sacred place by the Lakota Indians (you might remember Crazy Horse), who named the area "Paha Sapa," or Hills of Black. The color actually comes from the dark and dense pine forests that stand in front of the stony crags and canyons. Early French fur traders called it "Mauvaises Terres," or Badlands. The names stuck and are totally understandable from the back of a motorcycle—Jurassic ridges, canyons, domes, caverns, old mining towns, and more wildlife than the Bronx Zoo. I feel a bit like Alice in Wonderland when she ate the cookie that made her small. This terrain is not for the squeamish. It is the place where the dinosaurs and mammoths roamed thousands of years ago, and everything is on that scale.

Badlands National Park has 244,000 acres. I told you, it's big around here. The park is open for hiking, but the terrain off marked trails is treacherous and hard to follow. For once, we'll stick to the roads most traveled. Take a moment now, and wherever you're sitting, look about five feet away. Okay? Well, that's how close we were to buffalos as we rode past and among them on the bike. There are open range areas where the animals aren't fenced. Between that and the twist-and-shout ride through Needles Highway, my toes remained in the curled position all day. Other wildlife seen very close by are deer, prairie dogs, big horn sheep, marmots, woodchucks, cows, and horses. It's not like the Palmetto Expressway.

A visit to the Wild Horse Sanctuary placed us In an open buckboard in the midst of hundreds of beautiful untamed horses of every description, living naturally and protected on 11,000 acres. Some of them are adoptable. I resisted. Wow. All that, and it was only noon.

On a personal note, let me say that traveling with Craig is like having an enthusiastic housebroken T-Rex as a companion. He is tireless, fearless, resourceful, can sleep anywhere, eat anything, and he thinks I'm a really good sport. Even a T-Rex can be sweet. He even stops and asks for directions. I'm convinced that somewhere in his DNA there are explorers and bounty hunters.

Oh, before I forget, the drugstores here sell everything from nail polish remover to ammunition. We've bought both. Meals are very inexpensive—$6.95 for a complete dinner is common.

My beauty regimen now consists of four things: looking in the mirror to make sure my face hasn't fallen off, slathering on moisturizer, brushing my very straight hair (still no humidity here), and wishing I was thirty years younger. Actually, makeup around here looks very artificial, and T-Rex doesn't care.

There is much more to come, but the sky is blue. It's 70 degrees, and my toes have finally uncurled.

As always, love to you all.

Alexa
Aka Trailer Trash

Frank Lloyd Wright Collected Writings: 1931–1939, volume 3. Rizzoli, 1992. It seems originally published in the *Evening Huronite*, Huron, South Dakota, September 28, 1935.

Golddiggers and Close Encounters

We are still in Deadwood, SD. The truck needs some work. Great place to be, "stuck" in an area brimming with Old West history. Hard living legends died here: Wild Bill Hitchcock and Calamity Jane, to name just two. We have visited the Mount Moriah Cemetery, where they are buried. The irony is that those two despised each other in life and are now buried next to each other for eternity.

I had a great surprise in the cemetery. Up at the top, there is a Jewish section with headstones dated from the 1800s with names of prominent Deadwood citizens like Jacobs, Levinson, and Blumenthal. They were probably the merchants. Talk about wandering Jews!

Still haven't seen any synagogues since we left Miami, so I'm not sure if any of their descendants remain today.

As if Mother Nature hadn't done enough, man has added artful creations to these mountains. Mt. Rushmore is even more breathtaking than I expected. The granite faces tower 5,500 feet above sea level. Each head is as tall as a six-story building. From the brochure: "The faces appear firm, calm, confident and unchanging—a nice reassurance that things are fundamentally good in these United States of America, despite grim headlines." There is also a mountain carving in progress of Crazy Horse, the Lakota warrior who helped defeat Custer at the Battle of Little Big Horn. If the mountains were side by side, the latter sculpture would dwarf the former.

Now, to win the complete set of Samsonite luggage, who can tell me the names of the four faces on Mt. Rushmore, and who was Martha Jane Burke? Answers at the bottom of this message. No fair peeking!

Woo, woo! We rode on the Black Hills Central Railroad, better known as the 1880 Train. It followed along its original route between Keystone S. Dakota and Hill City. It was a nostalgic two-hour ride, complete with soot flying in our faces from the steam engine. Driving through the Badlands must be like being on the craters of the moon. No, I haven't been on the craters of the moon . . . yet.

It is a painting of prairies etched with sharp ridges, steep walled canyons, gullies, and colors. The bizarre terrain was formed inch by inch over millions of years, as wind and rain sliced into volcanic ash. Fossil beds are so plentiful that scientists call that epoch "The golden age of mammals." If I took a million rolls of film, I could never capture this exotic landscape. You'll have to come out here and see for yourself. Golddiggers must have gotten their start here. No kidding. The town of Lead, pronounced "leed," has the largest goldmine in North America and the third largest in the world. It was only shut down recently because during drilling they unearthed water and have been on the verge of flooding ever since December. We have seen hundreds of abandoned mines and more jewelry stores than Madison Avenue in NYC. The gold mines and gold rush of those days were responsible for the development of the town of Deadwood, which now has gambling. In fact, Kevin Costner has a beautiful restaurant and casino called the Midnight Star, right on Main Street. No, unfortunately, I didn't see him there. Are you worn out yet?

Next, we visited the mammoth site in Hot Springs (still in SD). It is one of the world's greatest fossil treasures. You might have seen the program about it called "Raising the Mammoth" on the Discovery Channel. The story goes like this: construction crews were excavating land for a developer when they uncovered the remains of a mammoth from 26,000 years ago. These enormous animals fell into a sinkhole and were trapped there and died. Because the bones they found are so fragile, they could not be moved, so the museum is built around them. Every year since the discovery, a group of people (just amateurs) come to continue the dig. Are you ready to get on the waiting list?

Last, but certainly not least, for today's report is the Devil's Tower. According to the brochure, "There are things in nature that engender an awful quiet in the heart of man." Devil's Tower is one of them.

We rode over the state line to Wyoming for lunch (doesn't everyone?) and followed the signs to the giant rock formation. In 1906, President Teddy Roosevelt proclaimed it the first national monument under the new Antiquities Act. It appears visually miles before you reach it—imposingly large and beckoning to come closer. It's a skyscraper that bloomed out of deeply ridged rock that has broken through the crust of the

Earth, rising 5,112 feet above sea level with a diameter of 1,000 feet at the base. Several Indian tribes have legends about this, but you would remember it best from the movie *Close Encounters of a Third Kind*. Try to visualize the ending. There were images of the mother ship from outer space, lights flashing, hovering over a gigantic, almost flat-topped form as it came close to landing on Earth. The form was the Devil's Tower, and in the skilled hands of a Hollywood director, the tower became a movie celebrity.

Answers to #1: George Washington, Thomas Jefferson, Teddy Roosevelt, Abraham Lincoln
Answer to #2: Calamity Jane.
Any winners?

Love to all, and remember: "Life is uncertain, so ride yer best horse first." —author unknown

Alexa
Aka Trailer Trash

Red Wigglers, Ghosts, and Moose Drool
June 2002

Today I had an epiphany in Cody, Wyoming.

I finally figured out how to get Craig, aka T-Rex, to go anywhere. All I have to do is post a big sign that says "road closed," "no trespassing," "enter at your own risk," "danger," and other similar forbidding messages. He can't get there fast enough. And here's how I know this . . .

We were just going out for a *USA Today* (an essential link to the real world when you're traveling the USA). The weather was becoming fierce. The wind gusts were already 40 to 60 mph, and snow was falling in Yellowstone and the higher elevations. I thought it was a good day to make soup and stay in the RV park.

"Want to go for a little drive?" T-Rex asked sweetly.

"Sure," I said, thinking in normal terms of fifteen minutes or so.

Two hours later, I was in Montana at 10,000 feet on a treacherous-looking road that eventually was marked "closed." Oy vey!

Because of the whiteout that blurred everything on both

sides, I really didn't know exactly where we were, but it was somewhere beyond Old Faithful, a few steps from Heaven, and everything was white. Craig was in his glory and would've driven on forever but for the heavy metal bar across the road. Thank God, whomever she is.

Now, you may be thinking, What a trooper! Isn't she a good sport? But during the two-hour jaunt, I could have won the Olympic nail-biting contest, and I did ruin what was left of a bad three-week-old manicure. All this while cursing the day I agreed to travel in a tin can for six weeks.

I must admit, though, in between the nervous nail-biting and cursing, I did manage a blurry peek at the extraordinary scenery that changed at every turn. And there were hundreds of turns. There were also blowing, howling winds, trees doing backbends, heights that would challenge a Wallenda, and the huge, ever-present, jagged, rugged, rocky peaks as a backdrop.

Later in the trailer, after kissing terra firma and sniffing nail polish remover, I studied my maps. I discovered that we had just driven along Beartooth Mountain (Rte. 212), the road that Charles Kuralt thought was one of the prettiest roads in the United States. You should read his book, *The American Way*.

Beartooth Mountain crosses the borders of Montana and Wyoming, passing rapid running (and chilly) creeks. It also encompasses the Chief Joseph Scenic Highway with valleys and in-your-face gorges. Oh, and did I mention that the sun came out on the way back to Cody, and I swear I saw every color of the rainbow in those mountain peaks?

The next day, in better weather, on a straighter, lower road, we once again went over the mountain—this time to Red

Lodge, Montana, a boutique Western town that reminded me of Aspen twenty years ago.

That is where I talked to Martha, a Montana local who raises red wiggler worms in worm beds. Of course, smart aleck that I am, I had to ask her if worm beds have down comforters? (No.) When you raise worms, do they go to college? (No.) And what kind of employment opportunities do worms have later in life? (Lots.) They are sent all over the world to landfills because they eat garbage—especially the mold on garbage. They are also a huge plus to coffee plantations because they're so good for the soil that the coffee grows in two years instead of three. And did you know that worms like music but prefer classical to rock and roll? So, all of you classical music fans are a boon to the worm population.

One more thing. Worms are bisexual, so all the red wigglers are totally datable. Worm woman Martha told me that she ships them to her buyer in Coeur d'Alene, Idaho, via US mail, in breathable bags lined with peat moss. The boxes are marked "live worms."

Want to work at the post office?

To complete my day, I dashed in to the Cellular One store and was greeted by an extremely geeky-looking guy with a Jim Carrey smile. He looked like he wouldn't hurt a fly. Wrong again! Geek guy Brian told me that a few years back he had driven a rocket launcher in Ft. Stuart, GA, and Baumholder, Germany. He was proud to say that he was raised on black powder muzzleloaders . . . originally Civil War rifles. I'm guessing he is not Jewish.

I also learned from him that in the old days, when fighting

the Indians, it took three minutes per round with this rifle, while the Indians had the advantage of five arrows to one rifle shot. When he started talking about the pig races in Red Lodge, I knew it was time to head for the bar at the old Irma Hotel in downtown Cody.

It is said that a ghost lives at the Irma, and after this trip, I'm willing to believe anything, so we asked . . . Where is the ghost? We were escorted to a large, old photograph hanging above the cherrywood bar that shows the Irma Saloon one hundred years ago. In the left-hand corner of the photograph was a white filmy image coming through a doorway, which did look exactly like a man with a white collared shirt dressed in the garb of the pioneer West. It was definitely *not* part of the scene in the photograph.

So, having almost touched Heaven and seeing a ghost all in the same day, I drank a Moose Drool and counted my earthly blessings.

Love to you all.

Alexa
Aka Trailer Trash

Btw, around here they say, "If you hear a click, hit the floor."
*Moose Drool is a very dark, creamy milk stout beer brewed in Montana. If you're a beer drinker, try it sometime—if you can find it.

Earth, Wind, and Snow... Where's the Beach?
2002

Just saw the film *The Divine Secrets of the Ya-Ya Sisterhood*.

We are in Cody, Wyoming, in a movie theater with wooden floors, where two popcorns and two drinks cost less than $4.00. Now, that's a "divine secret"! I loved the film and was only sorry that I couldn't see it with my Ya Yas. You know who you are, so start making your crowns.

Now, about the trip to Cody. This is Buffalo Bill territory, and getting here from South Dakota really tested my pioneer spirit and filled me with as much adventure as Buffalo Bill himself. I love the great outdoors; I just like it to be at eye level. To develop an instant fear of heights, just take Hwy 14 through Buffalo Bill State Park, Bighorn Canyon National Recreation Area, on to the Medicine Wheel Historic Landmark, Sheep Mountain Road, and Shell Falls. Looking out is gorgeous. Just don't look over and down. The truck and trailer climbed laboriously over the Bighorn Mountains, past Precambrian granite slabs dating 2.5 billion years ago. Snow patches, evergreens, and deer lined the rugged landscape. The temp went from 75 to 53 degrees in less than a half hour. It was an ear-popping, engine-straining experience, and our brakes were smoking and cooked before we finished. How would you like to come down from 9,300 feet with the smell of brake fluid becoming stronger and stronger? Every time I mentioned that I thought we were losing our brakes, T-Rex would say, "Stop worrying. And you are always smelling things. It must be a Jewish thing." Truth is, he knew darn well we were losing our brakes and didn't want to alarm me.

With the rig, we climbed up above the tree line, peaked at the top, and then the terrain started to flatten out. Praise the Lord and Craig's driving skills. Or maybe it was because I was clutching my voodoo doll (purchased in New Orleans) and whistling a happy tune that we made it safely.

Of course, the alpha male loved it—the steeper the better. With no brakes on the truck, we limped into the town of Grey Bull, which had a garage and not much else, and we had the master cylinder checked out. The fluid reservoir was full. No break in the line, no leaks, just too many mountains. We will continue on. The brakes will cool down, and yes, Mom, we're fine and currently able to stop the truck and trailer.

Cody is a real Western town. All the men carry guns and look like cowboys, even those wearing gold earrings. We have already seen a shootout in the street. It's a reenactment, but they used real guns and shot blanks. We had the fun of watching the Belmont races on TV in the bar of the Irma

Hotel, built by Buffalo Bill in 1909. The bar is all massive cherrywood and was a gift to Buffalo Bill from Queen Victoria. This night, it was full of drinking and smoking cowboys and girls who were there to participate in an event called "cowboy action shooting"—some sort of obstacle race. Every participant wore a gun and full traditional Western attire.

The weather is frosty, and it's snowing in Yellowstone, so we're hanging out in Cody 'til it warms up.

I've seen some fun names for businesses here like the Pony Espresso, a mini log cabin that you drive through for coffee. Mustard's Last Stand serves hotdogs every which way but healthy, and the Plush Pony is Cody's answer to Henri Bendel in NYC.

Let's all move to Wyoming. There's no income tax, four percent sales tax, only 500,000 people in the entire state, and you get to wear your leather jackets, boots, coral beads, fringe, silver, and turquoise that look ridiculous in Miami.

I'm looking forward to the ride through Yellowstone and warmer days.

Love to you all.

Alexa
Aka Trailer Trash

Thought for the day: "Take nothing but pictures, leave nothing but memories, kill nothing but time." (A caver's motto.)

Cody, Wyoming
Summer 2002
Bubbling, Gushing, and Swan Lake

Yes, Dorothy, cuddled between the cowboys and the cattle, there is culture in the West! The Buffalo Bill Historical Center, called "the Smithsonian of the West," is really five museums in one, and we spent the entire day there. We started in the Cody firearms section with over five thousand firearms on display. Regardless of how you feel about them, guns have been smoking through our vocabulary for a long time—like "going off half-cocked," "setting your sights," and "lock, stock, and barrel." It was hilarious for me to watch grown men drooling over a glass-encased Browning 50-caliber machine gun while their wives just rolled their eyes, probably wishing they were at the mall.

Next, we took a leisurely look at hundreds of beautiful paintings and sculptures, all depicting the West. After leaving the Russell's, Remington's, and Wyeth's (just to name a few), we went to the Draper Museum. This one takes you down an interactive trail of the sights and sounds of Yellowstone. It's the newest addition and would be sensational to experience with a child. I had T- Rex with me, so it was perfect.

Finally, the weather has cleared and warmed a bit. We are on our way to Yellowstone on the motorcycle.

This is the forest primeval, Yellowstone, the oldest of all our national parks. It is the size of Rhode Island and Delaware and sits in the northwest corner of Wyoming while part of it overlaps slightly into Montana and Idaho on the north and west. By the way, if you're a senior, you can pay a onetime, ten-dollar fee, receive a Golden Eagle Passport, and get into any national park free with a companion. Craig got one before we left, and it really works. Our grand loop started on a sunny but chilly 55-degree day with robin's-egg blue skies and snow along the sides of the road. We wore our full bodysuits, and I turned on the heated seat on the BMW motorcycle.

There were lots of people in the park, and I wished that there weren't. Somehow, all this humanity can detract from the sights. However, our grand loop took us past steaming, mammoth hot springs, a pond of gliding swans, and the world-famous gurgling upper geyser basin (home of Old Faithful). It erupted right on time, and humanity cheered! On foot, we were able to follow a wooden walkway around scalding aquamarine pools, where my sunglasses actually steamed up from the vapors.

Back on the bike, we toured Yellowstone Lake, meadows, forests, including the hundreds of acres that were lost in a fire in 1988 (and are making a beautiful comeback), snowy peaks, and the Continental Divide twice. I loved it, but little did I know that something even more breathtaking was just down the road.

We exited the park on the south end, which heads toward

Jackson, Wyoming. The reward at the end of the road is small in comparison to Yellowstone but one that I now consider a scenic highlight of this trip—the glorious Grand Teton National Park and the three peaks that look like Dairy Queen soft serve that are visible from Jenny Lake Junction. I was amazed and a little hungry from the sight of them. They ascend from the bottom of the valley, and they reminded me of the tapered spires and beautiful architecture of the Gothic cathedrals in Europe. This rivals anything I've seen in the Alps, so cancel your plans for Switzerland and head west! On our way back to Cody (we've motorcycled approximately 500 miles with an overnight stop), we visited Thermopolis, the home of the healing sulfur springs and the Wyoming Dinosaur Center. I'm feeling very young today, having spent the last forty-eight hours among 1500-year-old evergreens and 150-million-year-old bones. I'm feeling lucky, too, 'cause 150 million years ago, I would've been a small snack instead of a visitor.

Before the day was over, we saw the *Bourne Identity* at the fourplex in Cody and ended up in a cowboy dinner/dance club afterward. Cassie, the original owner, was a widow who ran it as a brothel to support herself, and from the look of the place, she was a success. At 10:00 p.m., the band started to play, and they were good enough to play at any bar mitzvah or wedding I'd ever attended. And then, much to my amazement, one by one, every man in the place corralled a partner and danced with the utmost confidence and grace. I was fascinated by the Western two-step. It looks almost like a waltz, with a quiet upper body and a swanlike gliding movement around the dance floor. The music changed from country to Carlos Santana and then Elvis. It was "Jailhouse Rock" in a sea of Stetsons and Justins—almost too much testosterone to watch. And then we danced, too. T-Rex was the only man in the room without a Western hat and boots. These guys are the real deal!

So long for now, pardners. It's on to Utah tomorrow.

Love to you all.

Alexa
Aka Trailer Trash

Go ahead, "Dance Like Nobody's Watching." Title song written by William Watson Purkey.

Dust Devils, Switchbacks, and Mormons
June 2002
On the Road to Moab, Utah

Moab is a biblical name. Apparently, before Lot's wife was turned into a pillar of salt, she bore him a son named Moab. Since everything under the ground around Utah is salt, maybe there's some connection?

Peculiar little whirls of dirt called dust devils are scattering around the landscape. They appear out of thin air and sort of flutter around like Earth clouds. Sometimes they're the only thing you see moving in the long stretches of wilderness. The ride from Wyoming is a long 400 miles, but we paralleled the Wind River Canyon, and once again, I'm awestruck by the beauty that is so different from Florida's. Huge boulders stand apart like stage curtains ready to showcase the show of slinky waterway and highway. We drive through ancient rock tunnels with rocks dating back 600 million years. It made me feel younger than ever.

I am also counting Wind River and its beautiful Indian legend (I'll share another time) in my top-ten-most-scenic list.

But wait. Now we're in Red Canyon in the Shoshone National Forest and are driving into a colorful wide stretch of coral. It looks like jewelry—a sparkling bright necklace of terra cotta and cream and is studded with shimmering emerald green brush and yellow wildflowers. Mother Nature was certainly not having a migraine when she did this one.

Uh-oh! Here comes a scary-as-hell 8700-foot-high pass, listing twelve switchbacks in 10 miles with a steep grade of eight percent. In a car, this would be exhilarating (maybe). Towing a 34-foot trailer, T-Rex has to work the trailer and truck brakes in all the up and down gear positions while, once again, I'm too scared to look out and enjoy the scenery. Among the views I do manage to take a peek at are flaming gorges, mountain reservoirs, phosphate mines, oil wells, and natural gas operations. All I can say after that ride is, no wonder the forests are petrified.

Still at 5,500 feet, we stop in Vernal, Utah, home of the dinosaur graveyards. I'm starting to feel like a Jurassic Park princess and am longing for flat land and sunshine. The next day, I get both. Even T-Rex didn't think our previous day's drive was a lot of fun, so we looked for and found an alternate route that took us over to Colorado and then back into Utah. It was flat and uneventful, and I loved it. I have concluded that in Utah, "Scenic Byway" is synonymous with "Scary Beyond Belief." The positive side of all this is that I'm too scared to get carsick. How's that for a silver lining?

They say that when traveling in Utah, you should bring your own CDs because all you will hear on the radio is country music, Rush Limbaugh, and the Mormon Tabernacle Choir. I'm well equipped with CDs and can pass for a conservative if necessary. Plus, I'm intent on hearing the choir in person.

Utah contains an unprecedented five national parks, seven national monuments, seven national forests, and forty-five state parks. It's also where Butch Cassidy rode a bicycle with the Sundance kid, where Max Von Sydow delivered the sermon on the mount in *The Greatest Story Ever Told*, and where Thelma and Louise drove off a cliff into a canyon. I can definitely relate to that one. It is also where the world's most famous automobile commercial was filmed (do you remember the car on top of a mountain peak)? And it's where Brigham Young took his twenty-seventh wife.

Utah has the highest literacy rate, the largest average households, and the second highest birthrate (thanks to Brigham and his followers, no doubt). It also has the second lowest death rate—that is, if you survive the ride in. Moab is known as the biking capital of the world, and the main streets are full of European yuppies (mostly Germans), granola girls, and lots of super young people in really good physical shape.

Sometimes you shouldn't get what you wish for—i.e., warmer weather. Today, we hiked in Arches National Park at a 5,500-foot elevation and 106 degrees. The humidity is only eleven percent, but the heat is like opening the oven door on Thanksgiving Day—without the good smells. The arches of different sizes are ablaze with colors. Seeing the scarlet and gold scenery makes the heat almost bearable. We saw a lot of people stopping and staring, but I think they were just trying to catch their breath. My sea-level lungs were gasping for air, and I was even a little nauseous. How much fun can one Jewish princess have?

Next was Canyonlands National Park. It's the home of the

Anasazi—the ancient ones—and has a pristine serenity vibe, but to tell the truth, I'm running out of adjectives . . . or maybe they just don't do justice to what I'm seeing. We took an inspiring evening sound-and-light boat ride down the Colorado River. The dancing shadows performed on the rocks to the rhythm of the background music and narration of the history that is hidden in these canyon walls. One of the songs played was "This Is My Country," sung by—you guessed it, and so did I—the Mormon Tabernacle Choir.

When I think about how it has taken thousands of years for this area to develop, I'm reminded that we're all just a small speck in time and place. We folks can be very time conscious, checking our watches and keeping our appointments, but out here it's obvious that the Earth has a timetable beyond our own imagination and our Rolexes.

The beauty of this canyon country is that nature is apparent everywhere, and so our connection with it cannot be ignored. Without billboards, traffic, and all the city trappings that distract us, it's so much easier to feel part of our planet. Sounds corny? Maybe. But it feels really good, and the eleven-percent humidity doesn't hurt either for another good hair day.

Love to you all.

Alexa
Aka Trailer Trash

We're heading for Las Vegas next.

Hoodoos, Smokey the Bear, and Totem Poles

We're in Cedar City, Utah, just two hours north of Las Vegas. The weather sprints from 50 to 100 degrees in the course of a day, but it's mostly fair and perfect motorcycle weather. I've been riding with a full-face helmet because the wind, sun, and dryness are taking their toll on my 57-year-old babyface.

First, the hoodoos!

Definition #1: noun; a pinnacle or odd-shaped rock left standing by the forces of erosion.

Definition #2: verb; voodoo (of African origin); to cast a spell or cause bad luck.

In Bryce Canyon National Park, it's all about the hoodoos. They range in color from pale salmon to cantaloupe to bright red-orange. If the altitude doesn't take your breath away, the sight of these rocky skyscrapers will. As an early rancher said, "It's a hell of a place to lose a cow."

Riding out of the park, we come to Red Canyon with still more hoodoos, but these are vermilion. They call this area Color Country, and it does remind me of being inside a kaleidoscope. Zion National Park was next, and it's completely different in character. At Bryce, we were looking down upon the hoodoos; in Zion, you look up at vanilla and glowing copper boulders. Parts of the highway are cinnamon colored as we drive through a mile-long rock tunnel and around Kolob Canyon. Zion is Utah's most visited national park. It has over 800 species of wildflowers, 75 species of mammals, 271 birds, 32 reptiles, 8 varieties of fish, and the endangered Zion snail. It's a hell of a place to lose anything.

This area is also in danger of fire—much like what's happening in Colorado—and we've noticed scorched trees and other signs of recent forest fires. Some were started by lightning, but others were intentionally set by park rangers using a modern ecological practice called "prescribed burning." Smokey the Bear has been such an effective anti-fire symbol that it's hard to understand why forest fires are necessary. But here's what I learned . . . Fire is a natural process that plants and animals have lived with since the beginning of time. Smokey and his slogan have gone against the laws of nature, and nature has suffered. Meadows are being overtaken by forests, and forests become overly dense and breed insects and parasites. Natural fires always burned away dead wood. Now, stockpiles of fuel wait for firefighters like time bombs. So, what I've thought of as destructive is really a necessity. Sorry, Smokey.

And speaking of bears . . . I met a wonderful wood carver who makes totem poles with cutouts of eagles, fish, and bears. His work is so artistic that I asked him if he could draw, as well.

He said, "No, my chainsaw is my pencil."

We continue to meet all kinds of people with a variety of occupations. Here are a few:

A retired pipefitter/welder (70-ish years old) who is called out to construction sites in different states. He goes with his family, does the work, and then travels all the way home as a tourist. He was dressed in overalls and missing a few teeth but has seen more of this country than most of us.

Then there was the German couple, traveling on their BMW motorcycle they shipped over from Frankfurt. He was a fighter pilot in the Luftwaffe. They spoke perfect English.

Next, a retired mechanic who we met in a little town called Panguitch, Utah. Turns out, he grew up in Hollywood, Florida, and went to the same tech high school (Lindsey Hopkins) three years before Craig went there.

We also met a high school boy who works in an ice cream store and told me he was so bored that the most exciting thing that happened all day was when a bee flew in and he killed it.

And just one more . . . A woman from California who lives in Cedar City and breeds Egyptian Arabian horses. As a child, her father was an Airstream dealer, and she went on Airstream caravans all over the world. As an adult, she ships horse semen all over the country. Do you think there's a connection?

And now the good news! We went to a Gold's Gym in town. They are currently having the Utah summer games, and Craig entered the arm-wrestling event and won three medals. The bad news . . . Now Craig cannot move his right arm, so we may not be able to load the motorcycle back on the truck until he recovers. So, I may need a volunteer, or we may not be able to leave for Las Vegas tomorrow. I really don't care. This is a beautiful RV park, and the Mormons are treating us very well.

Love to you all.

Alexa
Aka Trailer Trash

Hoodoo that voodoo that you do so well!

"Like a Virgin*" in the Dicey Desert
July 2002

This, all-in-one day: Welcome to Arizona, the "Grand Canyon State, " and Nevada, "125 Years of Vision," and California, "The Gold Rush State"—and currently the RV mash unit.

T-Rex has his three medals and a broken bone in his right arm near his elbow. The very handsome George Clooney look-alike orthopedic surgeon says no cast is necessary, but he does have a snappy black neoprene elbow sleeve, a bright-blue sling, and scripts for pain medication. That's a joke. Sling Blade hasn't even taken a Tylenol and just laughs through the entire process. Sorry, but a Jewish guy would have immediately called for an air ambulance, his lawyer to sue the gym, and rested for the next six weeks. Let's not even mention the kvetching that would last for days. Maybe it's something in the deviled ham?

So, in spite of the broken bone, we're on the road to Las Vegas with T-Rex at the wheel of the truck. We left the Airstream and motorcycle behind in Cedar City. Nothing stops an alpha male.

Virgin River Canyon borders both sides of I-15 as we drive toward Las Vegas. It's as scenic as the national parks. We're literally driving through a solid wall of gigantic boulders. The river part is nonexistent since it hasn't rained in four months. So, don't curse the Miami rain. Since nothing grows without water, the farmers and ranchers here are really suffering, and the fires are front-page news wherever we travel.

We are approximately 300 miles from Salt Lake City, and the posters of the missing child Elizabeth Smart are everywhere. On a vacation like this, you can only disconnect so much from the news, missing children, fires, and Martha Stewart's stock boo-boo kicking you right in your Zephyrhills.

The second we cross into Mesquite, Nevada's first city coming in from the north, we are bombarded with signs for playing bingo and slots from dawn 'til you run out of money. The resort gambling atmosphere is everywhere on the billboards, every one hundred feet, with casino names like Oasis, Casablanca, and Castaway. Wonder what the Mormons think of all this?

I think it's a nice change of pace. Since Craig flies to Vegas at least once a month for his company, I've been there recently, we're not gamblers, and the traffic is more than a full house, we drive right through Vegas across the Mojave Desert. I get to see the world's tallest thermometer, which is currently sizzling at 113 degrees but can go up to 130. We stop in the San Bernardino Valley, and the temp drops down to the 50s. Who can keep up with this? We're on the LA freeway, and it looks more like a smog-silly octopus. The traffic is beyond rush hour in Manhattan, and it's only 8:30 a.m.

It took us as long to go from San Bernardino through LA to Santa Monica than it took to drive from Utah to California.

And there are people who do this every day. Road rage to the max! However, it is nice to be in a city again—Rodeo Drive and all the goodies—pretty people, juice bars, Porsches lined up like cookies on a tray, and manicures and pedicures (yes, I got a wonderful perfect twenty from two Vietnamese girls at the same time). Now I understand why the guys go to Bangkok.

We visited some of my parents' oldest friends, a couple in 90210 (Beverly Hills). He'll be ninety in January and was an Academy Award winner for writing the screenplay for *From Here to Eternity*. She is blonde, aloof, and très glamorous, and they are both still super sharp and interested in everything. That's inspiring for whatever the future may bring for us.

Next, the walk on Venice Beach, aka Muscle Beach. It's a weird version of the Hollywood Boardwalk in Florida, but I love seeing the mimes, street artists, bodybuilders, a Michael Jackson impersonator, your name written on a grain of rice, and even a *Bride of Chucky* stuffed doll.

On to Laguna Beach to see my friend from high school. Laguna has the weather, the flowers, the walking paths along the beach, and lots of art galleries. I'm adding it to my boutique city list, and I could've stayed there a lot longer, but . . . time to go north to the PCH—Pacific Coast Highway.

Santa Barbara is trendy and the place where movie stars go to escape. I could have stayed there longer, too. Then, what a beautiful drive through farms, ranches, mountains, and little towns all running parallel to the Pacific Ocean, which takes turns lapping and crashing up against a caramel-colored beach. Wow, I really like this area. But what's not to like? There are acres of farmlands growing lettuce, broccoli, cauliflower, and strawberries everywhere. We stop at a strawberry stand, and I buy a pint of the most luscious looking and tasting berries, ever. The fruit-stand lady washes them for me and piles on a few extra ones. She thanks me profusely, and they only cost a dollar. At home, in fancy markets, they would've been $7.50, minus the muchas gracias.

Next, we visit the Madonna Inn that boasts the most interesting bathroom in the world. Not having been in every bathroom in the world, this is hard to validate, but the urinals are pretty amazing—especially if you like a waterfall cascading down, or a copper waterwheel turning while you pee. Beware if you're bashful. Tourists with cameras are likely to intrude. It also has a dining room covered in shocking pink on every surface. A real royal blush or flush.

The inn is a motel, and every room is decorated with a different theme, which are all incredibly kitschy. The place is incredibly gaudy, but it's lovable in a stuffed animal sort of way. We end the day in San Simeon and will tour the Hearst Castle tomorrow. Finally, the princess will be in her element!

Love to you all from castle country.

Alexa
Aka Trailer Trash

*Title of Madonna song

Whale-Watching, Wine Tasting, and Brothels

They are out there! Along the coast of the Pacific, big blues and greys blend in with the rocks—and who could see that far anyway?—so we investigate a whale-watching excursion. Just my luck (not really), this is the wrong time of year for whale migrations, so in order to catch a faint glimpse, you have to go out really, really far, on a very small boat, in rather high seas, in rather chilly temps for five hours. Damn, I've missed the chance to be freezing in the roiling ocean halfway to Alaska. Instead, I must suffer with an exquisite lunch perched high in Big Sur, overlooking the pounding, navy blue Pacific Ocean.

Wildflowers are everywhere. I lean upon purple and pink cushions and inhale cool sea breezes. Oh, well. A girl's gotta do what a girl's gotta do.

It's gorgeous on the Pacific Coast Highway. This is John Steinbeck country and home to familiar names like Esalen Institute, Monterey, Carmel by the Sea (Clint Eastwood was the mayor there at one time), and then up to San Francisco. But we're not going there. The fog does roll in on little cat feet, and it stays misty 'til almost 11:00 a.m. Sort of reminds me of the Italian Riviera without the gelato. I knew I'd reached a highly civilized area when I saw a Lexus with a license plate reading "to z mall." Now, why didn't I think of that? I also encountered my first gas station with a wine cellar. California is so trendy.

There is also a wonderful area called Paso Robles, featuring over fifty wineries. That's even more than I could take in in one day. However, we managed to stop at some of the prettier ones and have a taste or two. SummerWood Winery was especially picturesque in a Tuscan way, and their Syrah was delicious, so we bought a bottle. There is such a paradox here on the landscape, with cows grazing right along the ocean and then the mountains on the other side. My question was, do cows that live near the ocean give salty milk? Or are they just better swimmers?

In my opinion, California requires a separate trip—several weeks, at least.

It's hard not to notice the special California light that I've heard about from photographers and artists. At certain times of the day, the hills actually look like chamois or suede, and they glow. I'm buying a lot of postcards because my picture-taking skills are right up there with whale-watching. I have really enjoyed it here. Now, on to the Hearst Castle.

It always amazes and interests me to see what some people consider their life's work. In this case, the Hearst Castle is an example of a man who acquired great wealth and was influenced as a child by travels in Europe with his mother. William Randolph Hearst (grandfather of the infamous Patty) designed and built a castle that is more like a museum. To see it completely requires five different tours because it's so vast—270 acres, or the size of LA. The castle is set high up on a hill in San Simeon and overlooks the Pacific. It's surrounded by stables and peach, orange, and almond trees, to name a few. It makes Vizcaya in Miami look shabby by comparison. The most "enchanting" area for me was the indoor pool, which is half the size of a football field. It's completely tiled in small, brilliant-blue turquoise and lapis. The mosaic design covers archways and just about everything else. It looks like something out of *The Arabian Nights*. Hearst's favorite quote, and I believe the theme of his life was, "The best part about having a dream is sharing it." He would be pleased to know that more than 800,000 people visit the castle every year.

This is the now-I've-seen-everything paragraph. A drive-by and fly-in whorehouse. Come by car or by plane. These brothels are legal in Nevada and have names like "Shady Lady" and "Angel's Ladies." We stopped alongside the shocking pink buildings to take pictures and watched as a satisfied customer drove away. Brothel with a runway . . . Now, that's one for the books.

Love to you all. Have a safe and patriotic Fourth.

Alexa
Aka Trailer Trash

Trona, Death Valley, and Flip-Flops
July 2002

Erin Brockovich needs to go to Trona, Ca. I call it "the city that time forgot and that our government doesn't want to acknowledge." First of all, it's the last city before heading into Death Valley, so I expected a small oasis with food, water, lodging, and gas stations. Well, it has one gas station and five huge chemical refineries. The air smells putrid. Many buildings were abandoned, partially burned with broken windows and blown-off roofs. The people we saw (and there were few) all look like they met and married at a family reunion. We later found out that there are amphetamine makers living there. They can easily hide their illegal drug-making amidst the stench and debris. Obviously, Uncle Sam looks the other way in favor of the refineries. Believe me, there is nothing refined about them. This year, Trona wins my vote for worst city in the USA.

The heat is on! Death Valley is considered low desert with steamy, elevated temperatures. How about 120 degrees? But another low is the elevation—sea level and 195 feet below. Pretty good for a place with no water. You should know that the California deserts include Mojave, Anza Borrego, and Palm Springs. Among a million other things, they are responsible for Trail Mix and Twenty Mule Team Borax. Borax was mined from the area and hauled out by the tons—and the mules. Remember the actress Rosemary DeCamp advertising Borax on TV?

The desert is also where the sound barrier was broken for the first time in the world. We passed a large naval base around China Lake, where they do lots of secret things. Sorry, I can't tell you what they are.

The desert is where Charles Manson en famille hung out and where Elvis and Priscilla spent their honeymoon. We, on the other hand, picked the worst time of year to be here. That said (while sweating profusely in spite of the dry heat), Death Valley is gorgeous, and I loved it. I don't know the names of all the plant life or why the rocks are zigzagged with pink, violet, and gold, but the subtle beauty is memorable and the horizon endless. Could I become a desert rat? Not 'til winter when it cools off to 80 degrees. If and when I return, there is a spectacular place to stay called the Furnace Creek Inn. The totally unexpected elegance there is like something from the 1930s.

We have made the full circle back through Las Vegas. Here it looks like a national convention of sleazy tourists wearing flip-flops. I've seen more people here in an hour than I've seen in a whole week. The dancing fountains in front of the Bellagio are the only reason for me to be in Las Vegas. I'm sure some of you don't share my feelings.

I'll leave you with one bit of movie star trivia . . . Back in Paso Robles, we were on the highway in the exact spot James

Dean fatally crashed his Porsche into a 1950 Ford Coupe. It's at the intersection of Highways 46 and 41. He had received a speeding ticket two hours earlier for going 110 in a 35-mile-an-hour zone. The man in the other car survived and lived to be haunted by questions about the crash. His last name was Turnupseed. Just think if it had been Turnupspeed instead.

Love to you all, and drive carefully!

Alexa
Aka Trailer Trash

The North Rim, Route 66, and UFOs
June – July 4, 2002

The Grand Canyon! This is the Big Mac of all the sights we've visited. You can see it while riding a mule, on foot, in a helicopter, or on a raft. I can't possibly overhype it. The views literally take your breath away (especially after climbing stairs at 9,000 feet). The tourists here are from all over the world, and for the first fifteen minutes at the overlook, all I heard over and over again was, "Oh my God," or its equivalent in several foreign languages. I thought I was at some kind of orgy at the United Nations.

Did you know that the Colorado River cut and shaped the canyon, and that it's 227 miles long, and in some places, 6,000 feet deep?

Did you know that if you hiked from the south to the north rim (21 miles of steep trails) that you would pass through four of the seven "life zones" (a life zone being a region sharing the same climate, plants, or animals) found on the North American continent? Kinda like traveling from the low deserts of Mexico to the Canadian woods up north.

The north rim is less accessible than the south, so of course we (T-Rex) had to go to the north. Actually, I'm glad we did because there are fewer people and I felt that I'd like to have some private time with the views. I'm bringing back a full-color booklet because there is no way to describe the vastness and variations of colors I saw. One more thing . . . In 1979, the Grand Canyon was named a world heritage site, along with Victoria Falls in Zimbabwe and the Great Barrier Reef off the Australian coast.

It's the Fourth of July, and we're in Kingman, Arizona. For the first time in nine weeks, we're heading east—slowly—toward home. I am ready! This has been wonderful, but it's a really long time to be away. I've also decided that there is something like "tourist burnout," which I think comes from taking in so much and being in so many different places. Or, maybe there's just not an unlimited supply of "oh my gods" in a person's psyche. However, our return trip will not be without adventures. We're heading for Roswell, New Mexico, where there is a UFO convention this weekend. If you don't hear from me ever again, just look up and wave.

In Arizona and New Mexico, we traveled along legendary Route 66, most of which is now I-40. I didn't realize that it was the country's first two-lane road linking the shores of Lake Michigan and the Pacific Ocean, actually dead-ending on Santa Monica Blvd. There are just a few of the old landmarks left along the way, and I'm getting my kicks " . . . on Route 66" (1946 hit song sung by Nat King Cole, Chuck Berry, and the Rolling Stones) as we pass them: the mile-wide meteor crater, a wigwam motel with teepees instead of rooms, and old cars and diners. Another song by the Eagles, "Take It Easy," has a verse in it— a town en route called Winslow. Much to Craig's chagrin, I'm singing what I remember. It was pretty cool when we drove right past Winslow. I think he sped up just so my singing would end.

Love to you all. Hope you had a good holiday. It's so cool here tonight, we won't turn on the AC in the Airstream. I'd better enjoy it while I can.

Alexa
Aka Trailer Trash

The Roswell Incident
Roswell, New Mexico

According to our history books, Independence Day celebrations in 1947 were marked by events of cosmic magnitude. On that infamous day, intense thunderstorms demonstrated the power of the heavens. Amidst a blinding rain and an electric-filled sky, radar tracked an object falling towards Earth. Rumors of debris-strewn fields and military cover-ups suggested a UFO had crashed in the Roswell area. The mystery of the Roswell incident is still unsolved and attracts thousands of tourists every year. Is Earth the target of galactic probes, or is New Mexico simply an "out of this world" place to vacation?

Whether you're a believer or a skeptic, Roswell is the mecca for ufology. The aliens are everywhere we go. We've had "close encounters" at Walmart. "We've come to shop." We've seen Bullocks Jewelry Store, where they sell "unidentified flashing objects." Ate at a restaurant called "The Crash Site Café." Even the Super 8 Motel has a sign that says "Come Crash with Us." It's the funniest, campiest thing you can imagine.

To make it even better, we just happen to be here during the annual UFO convention. I haven't seen this many weird people since going to Fantasy Fest in Key West, FL. Even if the truth isn't out here, everybody else is, and a lot of them have green antennas and very small hands. There is a whole schedule of events. The electric light parade last night consisted of about five homemade floats and a lot of stray aliens wearing everything from cowboy hats to hula skirts. It makes hometown parades, like the wacky Mango Strut in Coconut Grove, look like the Rose Bowl.

Other events include a 5k alien chase, lectures by various believers, an alien marketplace, fireworks, an alien masquerade ball, and shopping. They sell everything from alien back scratchers to alien salt and pepper shakers. But here's the big one . . . the alien costume contest.

One of the judges was Dee Wallace Stone (she played Elliot's mom in *E.T.*). All the judges were dressed as extraterrestrials, and I can only hope my phone photos come out well. The contestants ranged from scary cone-headed space monsters to a group of senior Ya Ya aliens. There was an alien Elvis "Don't be fuel," a mistress Draconia with a knockout body painted in gold and sparkly stuff. The Ya Yas were in their seventies, and they had everything you can imagine hanging from their hats. They said they were from the planet Z-Ron because "Nobody else would have us." When interviewed, alien hobbies included mutilation and building bird feeders. I'm telling you, these people have made "contact," so we decided to get the hell out of there before we were abducted—but not before we made several tacky purchases at the UFO Museum gift shop.

Aliens will be a hard act to follow, but we plan to go to Carlsbad caves tomorrow. I can hardly wait, as I have already read about the much-heralded bat flight that occurs there every a.m. and p.m., as well as the ever-increasing tarantula population. Something else to live for.

Love to all of you. Still havin' fun.

Alexa
Aka Trailer Trash

Bats, Water and Trees
July 2002

Here's a comforting thought: There are about nine hundred species of bats in the world today. (A little factoid, in case you didn't have enough to worry about.)

If you want to avoid them completely, go to Antarctica, the only place on Earth they do not live. If you want to see fifteen of the nine hundred species, visit Carlsbad Caverns National Park. If you only want to see two of the fifteen species in the park, stay in the cave area. If you don't want to see any of them, but Antarctica is a bit too far, then you've got a problem. I settled for two but actually didn't see any at all. They are nocturnal. They leave the caves early in the morning and don't return to the caves until evening. But I learned a new term: *bat guano* (bat poop). And I also need to tell you, they are *not* blind. They have eyes and can see. So, from now on, you'll have to be as blind as something else. By the way, *guano* was used for years in the citrus groves of California as fertilizer. Have you had your orange juice today?

To see the caves, we descended down in an elevator 850 feet below ground. Down there, it's cool and dark. If not for the placement of lights, we would've been in total darkness. I was starting to feel blind as a ___. (Think of a word if you can.) The self-guided tour took us along a paved path with side railings. The almost two-mile walk is mostly level, with just a few steep places. The caves are beautiful. I finally know the difference between a stalactite and a stalagmite. The "tites" hang down from above, and the "mites" stand up. The nearest description I can give you is a sandcastle, fourteen football fields big, with all kinds of dripping formations. Some look like animal shapes, some look like draperies (and they are called draperies), and some look like domes. You can use your imagination, but whatever you see, it is a totally wonderful experience, unlike anything else.

*Ready for a riddle? What do you get when you cross a bat with an ice cube?

Most of the past two days have been spent driving through New Mexico, Texas, and now Louisiana. I get a little antsy sitting in the truck, but we stop a lot and have a lot of snacks. Crossing into the Bayou Country around Lafayette, I saw the first green trees and waterways that I'd seen since May. I was thrilled. What a contrast to the big naked boulders and scrub brush of the West. We stopped in Houma, LA, and toured a real plantation, then just poked around the area and drove the scenic route, which is Highway 90. It's slow, but it's raining on and off, and that's something else we haven't seen in a long time. Probably be home within a week. I'll be in touch.

Love to you all.

Alexa
Aka Trailer Trash

*Frostbite

August 2002
70 Days on the Road. The Conclusion.

As we approached Florida, we decided to take the "Forgotten Coast" instead of I-95 or 75—two of the most boring highways I know. The nature coast is actually the west coast/panhandle of the state. Traveling the Gulf Coast Highway 98 is like taking a trip back in time, probably no farther than the late 1940s and early 1950s.

There are small fishing towns, miles of undeveloped land, stilt houses along the water, and not a mall or fast-food chain in sight. This is the Florida I remember as a child on road trips in the family station wagon.

I'm finally back in the humidity, and the heat and thunderstorms are threatening. I'm loving it. We're almost home, and I'm happy about it. T-Rex is already starting to grumble about the lack of mountains and cool air. Are we geographically mismatched?

We find an RV park right on the water's edge, which is magically without mosquitos or no-see-ums. The breakfast menu at the local bagel shop (not really) includes eggs with chopped mullet. Do you get the picture?

After an engaging talk with the owner, he gave us two mugs with the restaurant logo on them as a present. Big red crab images on white mugs will now hold my morning coffee. Big lesson relearned today: Just because someone is wearing torn suspenders and a stained checkered shirt doesn't mean he's uneducated or unsuccessful. But of course, you all knew that. Our crab mug-giver, in spite of his appearance, was none of the above, except I didn't give him the best-dressed award.

The charm of small towns is irresistible, and it seems that the people living in them are happier, more content with their lives, and certainly more congenial. Everyone knows everyone else, and when help is needed, the townspeople just show up with whatever is necessary. No one needs to ask. On down the road, we pass through Apalachicola, Carrabelle, and Cedar Key. We notice a small roadside marquee that says "When light is flashing, we have live crabs." It's the Krispy Kreme of the Florida coast. I'm sure going to miss all of this!

The last few hours of our adventure are spent in the truck, and I have much time to process, evaluate, and form some conclusions about the whole experience. First and most important is that I had a wonderful time and would do it again. In the big picture, I would have to agree with Charles Kuralt. He often observed that this country was not in ruins and that there are lots of decent people living here, aside from crooks, politicians (or is that one and the same?), and pop stars.

That being said, I would also suggest that it wouldn't be a bad idea for all of us to get in a car, a camper, an RV, or a motorcycle, and hit the road. Stop and sip a Slurpee or eat an ice cream cone in a small-town gas station and make some conversation with some Americans outside of your immediate zip code. Our country is not in shambles. I feel reassured that it's full of beautiful places and good-hearted people who seem to have an endless desire for going God-knows-where, for God-knows-what reason, on anything with wheels and an engine.

I credit the American West for our most exciting history. Think about how bland our history would be without the cowboys, Native Americans, goldmines, canyons, mountains, and deserts. I credit the South for its slower pace, for retaining many of the gracious old-fashioned customs, for an ingrained politeness, and in a few areas for still wanting to fly the confederate flag, with which I strongly disagree. I credit the Midwest with down-to-earth people living happily in some of the most monotonous landscapes, which seem unbearably ordinary in contrast to the rest of the country.

We did not go to the northeast at all, but we know it's unlike any other part of the country with its own important contributions to our history. Maybe next time, although I doubt it, because T-Rex inherited a dislike for northerners from his very Southern-born mother.

Based on scenery, attractions, road conditions, and people, I would have to name South Dakota as my favorite state and Louisiana as my least favorite. Other observations include: Country music prevails and always comes in loud and clear in all regions. Dairy Queen has the most stores of any fast-food chain. Best breakfast is at the Cracker Barrel. Best healthiest fast food is Wendy's oriental chicken salad and baked potato with broccoli. Best motel is the Best Western. Most expensive gas was in Big Sur. Best-looking people are in California.

Worst-looking in Missouri. Cleanest city is Cedar City, Utah. Dirtiest city is New Orleans, LA, and Trona, CA, a close second.

We were never disappointed in any of the tours we took, attractions we paid to see, or national parks we visited. All were worthwhile and extremely well planned.

On a personal note, I had a lot of envelope-pushing to do . . . and reasons to go on this kind of adventure. Here are some of the questions, challenges, and results:

To see if I could feel at home in a world away from all things familiar . . . and I did

To break routine. And I have determined that monotony is the enemy to my well-being.

To make sure my world wasn't getting too small and without travel.

To appreciate the things I left at home. I missed my friends, my mother, the water views, dressing up, the buzz of Miami Beach, my apartment, and knowing where everything is.

To expect the unexpected, never knowing what the day would deliver.

To learn new skills, new facts about American history and geography, mechanics and how things work, and to know my limitations.

To be a more adventurous eater. Well, I did taste rocky mountain oysters. Yuck.

To remain my own person in the presence of new situations and in the company of a very strong male personality. This became easier with each day.

To see opportunity instead of fear, which I've learned holds me back sometimes. Still working on this one. I don't like those mountainous roads and steep drop-offs.

Otherwise, there was nothing about being on the road that scared me, plus traveling with T-Rex is like having a personal bodyguard.

I learned to trust my instincts, to speak of them, and act on them. This was a plus when the trailer had a gas leak and T-Rex insisted he didn't smell anything and that it was my "imagination." It wasn't, and we had it fixed before we were asphyxiated.

I learned not to expect to love everything we did and saw.

So, I'm back with my sense of humor intact, even though my fingernails are not.

I've missed you all. Thank you for all your email replies, enthusiasm, and compliments regarding my email journals. Let's do it again real soon.

Love to you all.

Alexa
Aka Trailer Trash

P.S. Porta potties still make me gag.

Things hardly ever seen or heard on the road:

parking meters
rude drivers
Frappuccino
sushi
The "f" word
French poodles
nannies
martini bars
condos
homeless people
Spanish
Cubans, Haitians
facelifts
"Pay before you pump"
call-waiting
stylish clothes
steamed broccoli
rap music
a bathtub
palm trees

the Atlantic Ocean
car or burglar alarms
Ferraris
synagogues
cockroaches
delicatessens
a decent manicure
bagel shop
a foreign film
traffic
a symphony
crème brûlée
Bloomingdales
a bad day
heavy rain with thunder and lightning

Things often seen and heard on the road

hundreds of RVs, deer, antelope, buffalo
"Yes, ma'am," "Yes, sir," "You betcha"
cows, prairie dogs
natural blondes, sheep, goats, armadillo
numerous dog breeds named "bubba"
moose, wild horses
twangs and drawls,
log cabins, manufactured homes
fast food
pickup trucks

state lines
sideburns
snow barricades
country music
women working with heavy equipment
machinery on road crews
bad teeth
public restrooms
USA Today
Pro-life anti-abortion billboards
wide-open spaces
Walmart
tobacco chewers
barbeque
dairy bars, ice cream shops
pull-on pants, elastic waists
Border collies
gunshots
courteous drivers
"Are you a full-timer?" —refers to a person who has no home other than their trailer, camper, motor home. (we were part-timers)
front porches
Pacific Ocean
drought
forest fires
75 mph speed limits

2003

Groundhogs to Blame for Landslide

Now that I've got your attention! (This was an actual headline in the local paper.)

Hi, everyone.

It's day three, year two of Trailer Trash on the road. Florida is a humid memory, and Georgia is "on my mind." This, after all the great packing experience. For me, it was like a fire drill, and at the last minute, I just gathered up everything, hoped for the best, and ran out of my building and into the big truck. Craig doesn't understand why with a year to pack, he ended up waiting for me for three hours, and I still forgot stuff. It's a girl thing.

Our truck and trailer together measure 55 feet long. Not meant for parking at Bal Harbour shops. This time, we've added more than the basics to take along with us: a GPS street pilot, two cell phones, a small plug-in fridge, a Sharper Image back massager on the passenger seat, enough small snacks to start our own concession stand, and the best of all . . . XM Satellite radio. We also have enough ammunition to wipe out every monkey-pox-carrying prairie dog in the US.

Scientists can gather information from the moon with fewer instructions than the XM radio manual, but just after crossing PGA Boulevard, where the real world starts, anyway, I got it figured out. We can now listen without static or commercials to one hundred and one digital stations—comedy, talk shows, news, sports, oldies, rap, Broadway tunes, and even the old radio shows. So, no matter how remote an area, we'll have radio—maybe no cell phone service, but Jackie Mason comedy bits and *I Love Lucy*. I also discovered the *Truck Stop Ministry* station. Isn't it amazing? The truckers are looking for the Lord, George W. is looking for weapons of mass destruction, and we're looking for my cousin's vineyard in Dahlonega, Georgia. In case you're planning a road trip, go through Georgia, where diesel fuel is only $1.23 and premium is $1.39. No wonder we can afford this trip! We went through Florida on I-75, which is a lot less boring than 1-95. That's not saying much. How can you beat towns like Ocilla—where the annual sweet potato contest is held—or Andersonville, remember the trials of the Civil War, and the notorious prison? From the looks of some of the folks around here, there must have been a lot of escapees.

On to Dahlonega, Georgia, home of the first gold mine in the US. No, I never heard of it before, either. But it is a lovely, hilly, rural area, one hour north of Atlanta, which, thank heavens, we bypassed. The cousin's vineyard is called Frog Town Cellars. It's totally captivating, high on a hill with acres of grapes on the vines and college-educated cows in the pasture who have never been "mad" a day in their lives. The sauvignon blanc was as good as any I tasted in Napa, as was the cabernet. T-Rex is having a blast driving the super duty and playing with his six speeds and Jake Brake. He's a "gear jammer" now. He never ceases to be enthusiastic and constantly good-humored. Must be the mayo that he puts on everything.

After a great visit with my cousins, the Jewish vintners who proved that Southern hospitality is an actuality, we headed out of Georgia toward the land of the sky, the region of western North Carolina, located on the losing side of the Mason-Dixon line. In addition to roadside rednecks, this area has some of the country's best artisans: woodworkers, weavers, and ceramicists, as well as environmental activists and alternative medicine gurus. It's also the home of one of America's finest novelists, Thomas Wolfe. He didn't think you could go home again, but I'm on my way to Burnsville, North Carolina, my second home since my parents bought a farm there (no snickering) when I was eighteen. We will drive through Asheville, where the Blue Ridge Mountains meet the Great Smokies. By the way, Asheville, according to AARP and Rand McNally, is rated number one as retirement heaven. Soon the blue-grey silhouette of the mountains will be visible in the distance, and I'm happily anticipating sittin' on my porch in the cool air. I'm told there's big doings in Burnsville—pig pickin' and team penning this weekend!

So, just like Dorothy, I've clicked my heels (not high ones) and traded traffic, heat, and Spanish for 65 degrees and bubba burgers. Hope you are all well and happy and that I'll hear from you soon.

Much love,

Alexa
Aka Trailer Trash

P.S. Scarlett would never recognize Atlanta.

Clouds on the Lawn and Study in Contrasts

Early morning in Burnsville, NC.

There are foggy clouds on the lawn, a bird's nest in the berry basket on my porch, and a baby horse in the pasture. What a beautiful scene! It sure beats I-95 and a pigeon doing you know what on my terrace at the King Cole condominium. Though I've been here many many times and seen the gorgeous views and smelled the fresh scent of pines before, all that really matters is that I'm here now, enjoying it all. Maybe the real adventure isn't about going *Where No Man Has Gone Before*—the book by William David Compton—but in conjuring up something unknown from within ourselves, no matter where we are.

There are thousands of destinations that draw personal explorers away from their careers, cubicles, homes, huts, mutts, and yes, friends. But I think the call of the road is really about indulging our primal urge to know the world, and through it, our place in it. And I don't mean a Ritz Carlton, although I will be looking forward to that at some point.

Apparently, we were born to travel. That's why we're fascinated with the Discovery and Travel channels, not to mention foreign foods and exotic clothing. Studies actually show that the gene identified with exploratory and thrill-seeking behavior happens to carry instructions for building brain receptors that attract dopamine—a pleasure-inducing chemical in our bodies. Those with a high need for novelty, risk-taking, and stimulation have a long form of this gene, while the more risk wary have a short form. And my point? Study in contrasts. Craig, aka T-Rex, clearly has the "long form," and I, the short. If the road is long, he wants to go farther. If the peak is steep, he wants to hang over it. If it's raining, he wants to be out in it. So, yesterday, with threatening clouds all around us, we rode on the motorcycle from the top of Mount Mitchell, the highest elevation around here (6,250 feet) on the Blue Ridge Parkway, all the way into Asheville.

Evening approached, and it was raining and cool, and the road misty and twisty. From time to time, the fog blotted out visibility of the road and created poofs off the motorcycle's windshield. We do have excellent rainsuits, and we did put them on, but still, I wasn't entirely comfortable out of my safety zone.

Ours is a true study of contrasts. This was his idea of an absolutely pleasurable experience, while my short-form gene was working overtime to get back home where it was dry and warm and I could see more than a foot in front of me. Our adventure genes are not compatible, but I stretch mine a little, and he compromises, and in the end, we were both glad to have gone on the ride. I'm learning every day how being on the road with a type-A personality can transform, but it requires holding my ground, taking risks, and frequent bouts of making a fool of myself.

But we do live to tell funny stories about it, and in the process, the vision of who we are and what's possible changes. In spite of the discomfort zones, it also makes me count my blessings, and I do that daily because a lot of the people around here don't have very much at all in the way of material things or the leisure to have adventures. They are hardworking farmers and mountain people who don't have the time or inclination to compare their mates' virtues and compatibility score. They exude a feeling of authenticity here, plus much of the food is from the ground instead of a drive-up window or boutique market. And everyone says "Hello," and "How are you?" And they seem to mean it.

More another day, 'cause speaking of homegrown, I have a bag of fresh, juicy peaches waiting. I'm going to make a cobbler. Company's arriving tomorrow in time for dinner. Happy Father's Day to those of you who are and have. Wish mine was still here, but every time I come up here, I thank him in my thoughts for finding this place and making it ours.

Love to you all.

Alexa
Aka Trailer Trash

Time to Say Goodbye... to North Carolina

It's always been difficult for me to leave here, but there are miles and miles to go for the next adventures. For now, I'm saying so long to the men named Clyde and Floyd who spit and talk with a wad of tobacco in their cheeks. I'll say goodbye to overalls and "Yes, missy," freshly picked 'maters, and the symphony of crickets every night. Toodle-oo to the tobacco in the fields, and cheerio to the rocking chairs on every porch, including mine. Ciao to the chimneys with the smell of hickory wood burning, and adios to all the rabbits, squirrels, and birds who have frequented my lawn and skittered along the fence lines. And bye-bye to the indescribable stillness. Fare-thee-well to roads called Lickskillet, Possum Trot, and Hardscrabble, and to a town with no movie theater and no-liquor-allowed laws (thanks to the Baptists and bootleggers). I hope I won't be saying goodbye to the calmness I've felt after the second day. (It does take time to gear down, and I think we don't even realize the hectic pace that we all keep at home.) And wonder of all wonders... sleeping through the night.

In the meantime, we have added a battery charger and a fire extinguisher to the contents of the truck. All I need now is a cappuccino maker (decaf) and a traveling manicurist so I can stay away indefinitely. We have decided to head toward Aspen, over 1,500 miles away. According to the map, it looks like we'll go through Knoxville and Nashville in Tennessee, then western Kentucky, Illinois (just a speck), Missouri, the St. Louis area, Kansas, and then into Colorado. Guess I better get some rest, kiss the family goodbye, and pack up the truck. I'll be in touch and hope you will, too.

Love to everyone,

Alexa
Aka Trailer Trash

Just Passin' Through Tennessee, "The Volunteer State"

What is it about this area that makes me feel like I'm watching black-and-white television? Can't answer that right now because, uh-oh, the inboard right tire has gone flat on the trailer. T-Rex announces this discovery in the same cheerful tone as the Waffle House waitresses saying "Good morning!" He isn't upset or even slightly irritated. He immediately was able to find a Ford dealer (right next door to Lois's Country Buffet), and we'll have lunch while the folks at Rusty Wallace Ford do their thing. We pull over and start to unhitch the trailer from the truck, but again, uh-oh, the electric motor that raises and lowers the hitch just quit. Surely T-Rex will now bellow. But no, he goes straight to the bed of the truck and lifts out a two-ton hydraulic floor jack (the size of Montana), gives it a few dozen cranks, and lifts the hitch off the ball quicker than most of us could have uttered several dozen curse words. I don't know how he remains so calm. Maybe it's the bean dip. And speaking of food . . .

According to *USA Today*, the latest statistic is that 64% of Americans are obese. So far, finding a slim and/or fit person in

Tennessee is like finding an English-speaking person in Hialeah, FL. It could be that Newport, TN, is the source of this research. At Lois's Buffet, this unscientific theory is substantiated by item number one on the buffet line: honey-stung fried chicken, then smothered pork chops with biscuits and gravy, and blueberry fluff for dessert. Every man in the place was wearing a truck hat, and none of them have seen their feet in years. The food was delicious, and we washed it down with sweet tea.

Still waiting for the tire fix, we kill a little time at the John Deere Tractor dealership. We may never leave Newport, but if we stay, nearby there's Dollywood, Pigeon Forge outlet mall and enough fudgeries to cause diabetes worldwide. Okay, the three-inch stainless steel screw has been removed from the tire, and we've been checked out and are ready to roll. Lesson learned: have the right equipment, plus the brain and muscle power to use it. And be sure to travel with a T-Rex.

Uh-oh. We need an ark, and even Craig doesn't have one of those in the back of the truck. The rain is nonstop, and traffic has stopped. We are on the interstate near Knoxville, and oh my God, two 18-wheelers (that's trucks, for you city folks) have flipped over down the road ahead of us. The only good news is that we can go inside the Airstream for the next two hours and use the bathroom, get stuff to read, and eat Oreos. The bad news is the slower pace of the South has come to a dead stop. We ain't movin'!

More good news. We can turn our clocks back one hour, and when we finally get moving, it won't be dark. The bad news is the traffic jam just got longer.

Signing off. I'm going to see how long it takes to lick all the white creme center off an Oreo and then eat the chocolate cookie parts. And yes, you can try this at home.

Love and patience to you all.

Alexa
Aka Trailer Trash

Sunflowers, Chuck Berry, and the Longest Day (Not the Movie)

If anyone would've told me we would've traveled from St. Louis to Aspen in one day, I would've told them to increase their medication and call me in a week. (Read on to find out how I almost lost my sunny disposition after sixteen hours in the truck.)

The longest day started at 7:00 a.m., right outside of St. Louis. I'm not going to elaborate on St. Louis too much because we really didn't spend any time there, but the Gateway Arch is quite a thrilling sight, visible and impressive from almost anywhere in the city. You should also know that at the 1904 St. Louis World's Fair, hot dogs, and ice cream cones were first introduced to the world. It's the home base of the National Bowling Hall of Fame, as well as home to *Wild Kingdom* host, Marlin Perkins. T.S. Eliot and Yogi Berra were born here, too. But the two things that make St. Louis a standout for me are these: #1, Anheuser-Busch's Headquarters. The brewery sprawls over seventy city blocks. That's a lot of ice-cold beer. And #2, and the best of all for me, the home of rock 'n' roll founding father, Chuck Berry. Though Eliot may have been an icon of Webster's English and intellectual ideas about American culture, for me, Chuck Berry ranks way up there as the lyrical/musical poet of what was happening in the '50s and '60s, i.e., "Johnny B. Goode" and "Roll Over Beethoven." Apparently, I'm not the only person who feels this way because when NASA launched the Voyager 1, its time capsule contained three things: copies of our Constitution, the Declaration of Independence, and a Chuck Berry tape. I rest my case. Oh, and one other thing. Eberhard Anheuser was a soap manufacturer who lent money to a failing beer maker. When the brewery went under, he took it over, hired his son-in-law, Adolphus Busch, as overseer, and renamed the brewery Anheuser-Busch. Wish I had a couple of cold "suds" right now.

Goodbye to Missouri, and hello to Kansas. It only seems quick because you're reading, not driving.

So now we're in Kansas, all day, and perhaps for the rest of my life. First of all, I think it's weird that Kansas City is in Missouri instead of Kansas, don't you? Second, Kansas is the Sunflower State, and I haven't seen one sunflower. What there *are* a lot of are farms, antique stores, oil wells, and wineries. Kansas earns the award for unending flatness and very strong wind currents. We can feel the wind buffeting around the trailer as we go. We've passed Leavenworth and Topeka and are paralleling the Santa Fe Trail west to Dodge City. Remember Bat Masterson and Wyatt Earp? They were great crime-crunchers in that wicked city.

Uh-oh!

We have another tire going soft, this time on the trailer. T-

Rex must be born under a lucky star because we find a "tarr" shop right away in Abilene (the Eisenhower Library is here, too). They change the tire in ten minutes flat. Oh, I better not use that word anymore.

Abilene is a cute town, and I have developed a fondness for places with one main street and lots of houses with porches. Everyone stares at us. Guess they never saw a six-foot-three guy in a Gold's Gym tank top or maybe it's my infamous beaded earrings? Onward we go, and how I sympathize with those pioneer women. This is the original long haul, and I'm not in a covered wagon. T-Rex seems hell-bent for Colorado by tonight, but I know that's impossible, so I just sit there and take it all in again and again and again. We passed forts, malls, and windmills. We drove on superhighways, two-lane creepers, through tiny towns and big cities. I've seen blue skies, thunderstorms, the plains, windstorms, and grey skies. The outside temp has jumped from fifty-seven degrees at 6:00 a.m. in MO, then up in the eighties in Kansas, and now fifty-one and dropping as we near Colorado. We've gone from 2,000 feet elevation to over 9,000 feet. I've seen John Deeres, real deer, hikers, bikers, and RVs. I am incredulous at the twelfth hour. Surely, we will stop and rest, but no.

T-Rex says, "I could drive for another four or five hours."

And sure enough, he did. Plus, he added that we had just gained another hour of "mountain time." The longest day just got longer! I was annoyed and tired and hungry. What's the rush? I thought if I'd wanted a stint in the Marines, I would've traveled with Uncle Sam. The Denver airport in the distance was a huge temptation, but I resisted. We drove on and on through a highway of winding mountains. I was unusually quiet (which usually signals discontent), and darkness was falling.

As we came out of Denver toward Aspen in a rainstorm, with the temperature hovering right around fifty degrees, the clouds suddenly cleared, and a double rainbow appeared right on cue. It was our welcome to the Colorado Rockies. It was such a vibrant arc that I even saw the purple band, which is usually just a shadow. This, however, was only a momentary distraction from the fact that I had been sitting in the truck for fourteen hours—give or take a few rest stops and a flat tire. I know that my Jewish Hall of Fame award will be waiting for me when I get home, but right now, it would be nice to have just one sunflower and my pillow.

If you're getting weary reading this, try to imagine doing it. The last draw was that every place that serves food in Basalt and Carbondale was closed by the time we arrived, so I went to the 7-Eleven and got a banana and some cottage cheese. Most unsatisfying!

It was midnight by the time we got to the RV park. The office was closed, and though they had left our reservation pinned to the screen door, it was so dark and tree-filled in the park that we couldn't figure out where our space was. Finally, at 1:00 a.m., in the cold and windy night air, we were hooked up and settled in. Welcome to Aspen/Basalt, and goodnight to the longest day. I went to sleep with visions of private jets, Ritz Carltons, and sunflowers dancing in my head.

Love to you all.

Alexa
Aka Trailer Trash

P.S. It's been said that a healthy mind can find something positive in everything and everyone. That mind obviously never traveled with T-Rex.

The Color Green, Roadkill, and Altitude Sickness

Hi, all.

We've been in Aspen/Basalt for a week. Weird sightings and sayings along the way include: a shower curtain instead of a door in a restaurant lady's restroom (it wasn't exactly a four-star), a Model 23 Learjet parked in the front yard of a farm, a woman wearing a miner's headlight on the dance floor (clearly a lifetime subscriber to *Vogue*). As for the sayings . . . When we mistakenly discussed crime and the legal process back home, we were advised of the delight-my-day mentality—"We just take 'em out and shoot 'em around here." And that was from a well-dressed woman who owns a fine art gallery. Also, a sign seen in a cow pasture as we rode into Durango: "I'd rather be a cow than a condo." Now, that one has potential for home. And for all you healthy eaters: "Think globally, eat locally," which I do every time I pass a cherry orchard.

I feel a little like Kermit the Frog right now because I must comment on the color green. Last year when we were in the mountains of Wyoming and Utah, I found them barren of greenery, even as they were colorful in their own subtle way, and I started to long for the palm trees and lush foliage of

Miami. By contrast, Colorado mountains have every shade of green.

My mind wanders as T-Rex drives, and I mentally name the shades as we go—collard green for the Douglas fir, emerald green for the flecks of juniper and pinyon pine, Crayola blue-green for the blue spruce, evergreen, grass green, and maybe just projecting a little envy green for all the folks who are not here and are sweating it out in Florida.

As we drive, it occurs to me that in Miami, when something skitters across the road, it's usually a crushed can of Diet Coke or an empty bag of chips. Around here, instead of litterers, there are critters: skunk, possum, deer, coyote, elk, and itty-bitty prairie dogs. Lots of them don't make it across and become roadkill, or maybe beef jerky, but we also had to stop short for two agile deer who bounded out in front of us and then gracefully leaped over the nearest fence. It sure beats a drive-by shooting.

Take a deep breath. There is less oxygen here. (Approximately forty percent lower oxygen pressure than sea level.) In Telluride, for example, altitude is 8,750 feet. You've all heard about altitude sickness, and I hope none of you have ever experienced any of the symptoms: dizziness, nausea, headache, shortness of breath, trouble sleeping, decreased appetite, and thirst. It seems that fitness doesn't matter a bit. A sedentary slob and a triathlete have an equal chance of being affected. But our crafty little bodies cope by producing more red blood cells to carry oxygen, and in a few weeks, anybody's body will acclimatize. It's kind of a natural blood doping, and many athletes do train at higher altitudes for that reason. The locals advise less booze, more water, and 100 milligrams of ginkgo biloba, two times a day, starting five days before arriving at the high altitude. There is also a prescription medication called Diamox. Personally, I feel fine, but even one glass of wine packs a wallop, so finally, I am a cheap date.

Love to you all, and enjoy the air at sea level.

Alexa
Aka Trailer Trash

San Juan Skyway: Aspen to Ouray to Telluride to Durango to Silverton Or "The Loop," Part 1

Question: At 10,640 feet, with a drop as sheer as your best Hanes, why aren't there any guardrails on these roads?

Answer: Guardrails would block the snow from being pushed off the highway by the snowblower machines. This, of course, makes me a lot more comfortable going around the hairpin curves. We have left the Airstream parked in Aspen/Basalt and are taking the truck to go around "the loop." The locals call this state "Colorful Colorado," and the stunning ride along the San Juan Scenic Byway proves the name with rusty-colored bluffs and golden aspens at every turn.

Our first stop is Redstone, known as the Ruby of the Rockies. It was love at first sight for me. This is a nano town full of galleries and craft shops. Everything on the only street is displayed outside, so I feel like I'm walking through a community art show.

We had breakfast at the historic Redstone Inn (1893) and an unexpected meeting with Sterling Hayden's son, Paul, who lives in Aspen. For those of you too young to remember, Sterling Hayden was a very popular movie star. He played in the films

Asphalt Jungle and *Johnny Guitar*. Back on the road and over McClure Pass, the next big stop is Ouray, called the "Switzerland of America." I wouldn't go that far, but it is a charming though spartan town. It has steep, unpaved streets that are full of Victorian hotels and shops, plus a public hot springs pool where you can "take the cure" while looking up at frosted peaks. It was named after a Ute Indian chief, Ouray. There are hundreds of bikers, bicyclers, and four-wheelers, but I did feel like I was walking where hooves and moccasins had gone before.

We continued on the Million Dollar Highway, one of the most dangerous roads in America. We passed Montrose and took a shortcut through Dolores and Ridgeway, the town where *True Grit* and *How the West Was Won* were filmed. We're on the way to spend the night in Telluride but may never get there because we keep stopping to take photos. This has got to be one of the most scenic and varied rides in America.

We got there! Telluride is a Western version of a fairytale come true. Colorful clapboard houses, gingerbread architecture, and big fluffy dogs dot the one main street. Some people say that the name Telluride is a contraction of "To hell you ride," but this must be a reference to a rowdy past (Butch Cassidy robbed his first bank here in 1889) and its remote location, which must have been "hellish" to get to in winter. All that is changed with an airport that accommodates small private jets, and I know that the Miami Snow Ski Club has had trips here. This is a very popular destination for skiers, hikers, celebrities, and people who want to "find themselves." It's also a town known for festivals, wine, music, art, and even hang-gliding. People braver than I jump off the mountaintop at dusk. We watched them float down just as the sun was setting. The town reeks of understated elegance and wealth. The people were very friendly, and most come from somewhere else. They are very casual and hip. It's no surprise that real estate here has climbed higher than most of the surrounding peaks. We looked at a few homes in the two- to five-million-dollar range, just for the tell of it. Just looking!

We stayed overnight at the Sheridan Hotel, which is one hundred years old but has been completely renovated. It was fun to have a jacuzzi hot tub, modem access, and freshly baked chocolate chip cookies in a room that looked like a shady lady had entertained there. During dinner we saw a bright yellow Ferrari convertible (Spider) whiz by. It was Ralph Lauren. He and his wife Ricky have a ranch here on 14,000 acres. The T-shirt business must be incredible!

I hated to leave Telluride. If I could afford it, I'd spend more time here someday. One last look at Bridal Veil Falls, the longest free fall of all the waterfalls in Colorado (off a 425-foot cliff), and we're off for Durango. We have tickets for Friday in the open car of the famous Durango Silverton steam locomotive. Part two after the ride . . .

Love to you all.

Alexa
Aka Trailer Trash

P.S. One drawback to Telluride: I noticed some strange lock-down devices on the garbage cans in town. Apparently, the bears love Telluride, too.

Riding the Rail – Durango/Silverton
Friday, June 27

Steam . . . My day begins and ends with it. First, the steam rises from my morning coffee, and then steam on the track. The famous Durango Silverton steam locomotive is hissing and billowing. The steam rises over the bright yellow rail cars ready for their day's roll, and we hear the conductor's "All aboard!" We are in the open car. All seats are reserved. The route is 4.5 miles. I get to practice my Jewish princess wave as we pass people at the crossings. It's like a cinemascope of scenery—the lakes, the waterfalls, the suspension bridges, and the climb. The train works hard with constant chugging and spewing.

We pass the spot where *Around the World in Eighty Days* was filmed. Everyone leans out to see the big clouds of steam, and as we round the bend, I can see the front of the train now. Above us are the razor-sharp 14,000-foot peaks of the Needle Mountains. Silverton is within sight! This was once the stomping grounds of silver kings, railroad giants, and true grit. It's a place for people with a high level of tolerance for isolation and physical adventure. What am I doing here? Surprise, surprise. I like it. It feels authentically Western, with sidewalks still planked in wood, noisy saloons, notorious Blair Street (fallen angels and painted ladies worked here), and a main street that has a shootout every day at 5:00 p.m.

On the modern side, Silverton is the home to Colorado's Outward Bound School headquarters and an extreme ski area called Silverton Mountain. (I think this used to be called Purgatory.) This is a quirky and unpretentious town with a permanent population of only three hundred. We had no reservations (which I'm sure would make some of you uncomfortable), but we always found something, and this time it was an unexpected gem. It's called the Wyman Inn and is listed in the National Registry of Historic Inns in America. With a gourmet chef and a vacancy or two, we were all set. And then, we were given the choice of an elegant conventional Victorian room with antiques, a king-size bed, and a full bath, or for the same price, a night in the "candlelight caboose." Of course, you know we had to choose to sleep in an old-fashioned railcar—bright-red exterior, parked in a private gated courtyard next to the inn. The interior was beautifully furnished with a Ralph Lauren duvet and linens, a mini-CD player with all the classics, and a huge jacuzzi tub bordered with small fragrant votives. All of this diverted our attention from the bathroom, which was the actual toilet compartment from the Southern Pacific RR. Very small. Our unforgettable experience included sleeping amidst all the original metal pipes, an unacceptable shower, not enough hot water to bathe a flea, and a phenomenal breakfast. We did it, and we're glad. That night, we ate dinner at the Trail's End, full of some strange-looking locals and amber ales. For a moment, I thought I was in an episode of Northern Exposure, especially when I saw a woman on the dance floor wearing a miner's helmet and headlight! It's a long way from Lincoln Road. All aboard!

Love to you all.

Alexa
Aka Trailer Trash

Celebrity Sightings, Silly Names, and Characters

I forgot to tell you all about the ranch. This is the second home that Craig's boss owns in Aspen/Basalt. It's a real log home (two-story mansion) complete with a double staircase, wonderful Western art, granite counters, a stable, a separate guest house, motorcycles, dirt bikes, ATVs, skeet shooting, perfectly trained quarter horses, a hot tub, fireplaces, children, nannies, an occasional celebrity, and gracious owners. It sits on a magnificent 650 acres with gorgeous views everywhere. All that, and it's most comfortable and unpretentious. Honest!

We had just stopped by on the motorcycle to say hello, and on the way, I saw a parent hawk teaching its babies to fly in formation. A truly Audubon Society moment. Our hosts are always generous and hospitable, so we ended up staying for dinner. The good news—we ate fall-off-the-bone delicious spareribs and steaks with movie stars James Caan and George Hamilton. The bad news—I had helmet hair when I met them. I guess it wasn't that much of a deterrent because the next day they came by the RV park and hung out with us at the Airstream. They had to try riding Craig's BMW bike, and Caan dropped it right there in front of us. No damage except maybe to his ego, but he is a riot and full of energy and jokes. Hamilton is soft-spoken and perfectly groomed, even after horseback riding. Did I tell you that Paul Hogan, aka Crocodile Dundee, fills his propane tanks at our RV park? The owner here says he is exactly like his movie character. I'm hoping to catch a glimpse of him so we can compare knives.

Craig is a people magnet. Sometimes I think it's his height and demeanor, but this time it was his Area 51 T-shirt and license plate that attracted the local US Marshal (Norman, originally from Milwaukee). Again, everyone who lives here seems to have come from somewhere else.

Back to Norman. He stopped us right in the middle of town (Telluride) to ask a million questions about the secretive Area 51 and Nellis Air Force base. We were there a couple of years ago, when we were in Las Vegas. We rode outside of the city and into the desert on the Extraterrestrial Highway and stayed at The Ali Inn ("alien"). Norman's buddy, a llama rancher, had spotted us the night before in a bar and passed on the info. Small-town grapevines are juicy and efficient.

And then there was Andy, a retired eye doctor from Maui. Fit as a fiddle, bursting with enthusiasm, he "eyed" T-Rex, the truck, and license plate. Turns out he had been a fighter pilot, is now a photographer, and surfs five out of seven days with his wife. Oh, yes . . . and he's seventy-four years old. Maybe it's time to get off the couch and hang ten . . . or at least nine.

Next, we met the black (African Icelander) biker—yes, all the way from Iceland—then the six-foot-tall woman originally from Oregon who owned a gallery so upscale that she had pieces in it from an artist whose work is displayed in the Smithsonian. Last but not least is Tom, the proprietor of an inn, who lived most of his life in Asia, with a ten-year stint in Key Largo. Tom had a club foot, a roving eye, and probably a propensity for "peeping."

I'm feeling freer this year than last and talking to more people. Friendliness really adds to the adventures.

Just a few ideas if you are thinking of naming a new business:

The" Kum & Go" (the one-night stands of convenience stores usually attached to a gas station)

Pasta la Vista (spaghetti joint, Terminator style)

The High Noon Hamburger (Gary Cooper's favorite)

Dip and Strip (Solid Gold of a mining community)

And one more very familiar phrase: "No service," which has been appearing regularly on our cell phones—just where we might need them the most. In a remote place, they never work. I guess my cell phone plan doesn't include mountains and meadows. Maybe it's time for satellite phones and solitude.

I'm way behind in my trashettes, but there's not always time in my day to compose them, let alone have the opportunity to send them to you. Hope I'm not boring you with all this, but as I said last year, these messages are a great way for me to keep track of our trip. Thank you all for reading them and responding when you do.

Love to you all. Hope it's a booming, sparkling, patriotic Fourth. It sure is out here. I'll be in touch.

Love to you all.

Alexa
Aka Trailer Trash

"Wide"oming, The Cowboy State, the Oregon Trail, and More Mormons
June 30 – July 2

I should call it WOW-oming. This place feels like a bunch of small towns with long, barren stretches of road in between.

We left Colorado and drove out through Glenwood Springs, Rifle and Craig (those are towns), and toward Wyoming. Baggs is the first town across the state border, population 348, and not one of them is wearing a Ralph Lauren polo tee. Right out of the box, filling up the truck, we saw what we thought were two locals sitting at the Conoco gas station and staring out into space. Then they saw us, said "Nice rig," and one thing led to another as we chatted.

So, if I tell you again that you can't judge a book by its cover, you will think I'm being repetitive, but they turned out to be successful businessmen, semi-retired, one a funeral director, the other a dentist (hopefully they didn't work together), and both were from North Carolina. The fact that I judged them poorly because they looked like *Hee-Haw* rejects is not surprising. My frame of reference from growing up in Miami Beach doesn't include successful men in overalls. What was surprising is they told us they had trailered 26,000 pounds of building materials and a construction crew from the Charlotte, NC, area to build a house in a town that by all rights is lucky to exist.

Bottom line, people never cease to amaze me. Last year we spent quite a lot of time in Wyoming, Cody, the Grand Tetons, Jackson Hole, and Yellowstone. This time we're just going to use Wyoming as a path to Montana, but there's something I want to mention about the people we've encountered from there. Aside from the rugged beauty of the state's varied landscapes, Wyoming would not be what it is today without the cowboy.

Although typically individualists, cowboys also are most often willing to gather, to "circle the wagons," to join in a just cause, and stay with it until it's accomplished. It's the free and committed spirit of these freedom-loving people that I love and admire. Whenever I see something scary on the news involving America, the wannabe cowgirl in me thinks of Wyoming and appreciates this attitude of doin' it 'til it gets done even more. "Support our Troops" signs are everywhere in Wyoming, and I doubt any terrorist would last too long there.

We stayed two nights in Casper. The main street is dotted with life-size buffalo statues in artistic forms of color and theme, much like the 1999 Cows of Chicago exhibits. That was fun to see them standing still on every other block.

We also visited the Western Trails Interactive Museum. Each visitor follows in the footsteps of the pioneers and Mormons as they emigrated west on the Oregon Trail. The fabulous and realistic displays include sounds and sensations with film, touching and reading, seeing the clothes and cooking utensils, and hearing an oral history. Imagine riding in a bumpy covered wagon and sitting in a cramped stagecoach with nine other people inside (three more on top). I can only begin to understand the words *fortitude, hardship,* and *faith*. With all that these people endured, it may also have been the birth of the first anxiety/panic attacks. Parties started out with 800 people and ended up with 130. Not my kind of party. They died of cholera, childbirth, starvation, freezing temperatures, drowned, fell off the wagons, and were run over. If I had survived all of that, I think I would've been black and blue and then died of boredom.

We learned about the progress of communication and travel and how the telegraph put the Pony Express out of business after only nineteen months. And then the railroads changed everything, iron bands linking East to West. The Mormons were extremely disciplined and industrious. They were the first to think of using handcarts and wrote many of the guidelines for the travelers that would follow. They started the first ferry across the Platte River (which was three football fields wide, had strong currents, and was freezing most of the time), charging $3.00 a wagon. Maybe they were really Jewish.

It's hard to believe that we are so far from home—2,000 miles, according to our GPS. Since it measures in straight lines, it's probably even more. I'm feeling like a much more seasoned traveler this year with most of the mechanics of RVing mastered, but still bombarding myself with questions like how it can be ninety degrees out when I'm seeing snow-covered mountains across the road? And where do all these cows go in the winter when the snow drifts are fifty inches high? And where did the word *Mormon* come from, and who invented the railroad? I'll welcome any of your answers. Montana is next.

Love to you all.

Alexa
Aka Trailer Trash

Bathless and Battlegrounds

The Battle of the Little Big Horn is also known as Custer's Last Stand. Who or what is "Garryowen"? Well, it's an Irish song, and 125 years ago on June 26, it was the marching song of the 7th Cavalry Regiment. Why an Irish tune? Did you know that most of Custer's men were immigrants? And the largest numbers were Irish, then Germans, Canadians, New Yorkers, and Ohioans. Unfortunately, the "Luck of the Irish" didn't bring them a victory. We stood high on a hill overlooking the exact spot where the battle had taken place. Some say ghosts have been seen marching there, but we didn't see any that day. Probably gone off to the pub. The terrain is basically unchanged but for the white gravestones and a new peace memorial that was created this year to honor the Indians and their losses. "Peace Through Unity" is engraved on the monument. I tried not to put too much importance on the adjacent sign that reads "rattlesnakes on trails."

In Billings, MT, we toured the Moss Mansion (not my friend Flo's). This home was designed by the same architect who designed the Waldorf Astoria and Plaza hotels in NYC. The Preservation League ladies informed us that P.B. Moss was quite the entrepreneur, a banker, rancher, farmer, owned the power plant, built the hospital, built the first hotel in Billings, started the *Billings Gazette,* and still had time to father six children. My Stetson's off to Mrs. Moss, because even in the finest homes, a shower was a weekly luxury. How's that for a romantic endearment?

Craig's favorite thing in the house was the separate back stairs, leading to the servants' quarters. He probably pictured himself, years ago, sneaking up there and visiting with the scullery maid. Good luck to both of them, bathless and bawdy! I, on the other hand, loved the old rose wallpaper and the wooden butter molds. It must be a princess thing.

Thought for the day from Montana . . .

"If you don't stand for something, you'll fall for anything."

(Maybe from Alexander Hamilton or Peter Marshall.)

Love to you all. Fourth of July tomorrow!

Alexa
Aka Trailer Trash

2002 (or so), July 4th, Red Lodge, Montana
Sparkle, Pop, Fizzle, Whinny

I wondered, where will we be on the Fourth of July? I was wishing for a small town with big, patriotic festivities. Bingo! Between daytime in Red Lodge and nighttime in Laurel, I got an all-American Western version of Independence Day in Montana.

Red Lodge had a parade, antique cars, American flags, decorated horses, stagecoaches, motorcycles, cowboys and girls, big dogs wearing bandanas, picket fences, barbeques, and a modern-day version of Custer's 7th cavalry marching band in full uniform, which managed to visit every bar in town—and there are quite a few. The day sparkled even before the fireworks, with picture-perfect mountains and 72 degrees dry temperature. The little town was packed with people from nearby (Yellowstone, Cody, and even Billings). We checked out every store and saloon and even signed up for a silent auction in the art gallery. And when was the last time you were in an art gallery and heard a horse whinny? Right there, his head looking through an open window.

After the daytime festivities were over, we took a drive-up

Bear Tooth Pass, Route 212. Last year, that road was closed because of snow, so T-Rex needed to pursue and conquer the winding highway again. Prettiest road in America? Sure, it is, if you dare to uncover your eyes for more than a minute.

The surrounding mountains are shaped like huge teeth and are frosted with snow (or maybe it's Colgate). I was glad I had liked my lunch because it seemed I would be tasting it again soon. Twisting and shouting at 11,000 feet, I could feel my familiar fearful toe curl as the temperature dropped down from 85 to 52 degrees. Who the heck built this road? And now the tooth twists sharply and we're back in Wyoming and the Shoshone National Forest. Snow-sticks line the upper elevations so that in the winter, planes can fly over them and see how high the snow is. All I can say is, who really needs to know? It's July Fourth, and there's snow to the right of me and snow to the left of me. I need a snowmobile, not a Ford truck. In spite of my fear of heights and my slightly queasy stomach, I must admit it's absolutely gorgeous everywhere I look.

The day ended in Laurel, Montana, close to 10:30 p.m., when the sun finally ran out of shine, with the best fireworks display in the state. Pop, sparkle, dazzle, and boom rained down on us for almost an hour. The fireworks were choreographed to the music of Lee Greenwood's "Proud to Be an American," Neil Diamond's "Comin' to America," and several more heartwarming and stirring selections. Over 20,000 enraptured faces were tilted up toward the clear black Montana sky. What can I say—Old Glory was probably doing the two-step with the Statue of Liberty, and I was proud to be an American and thrilled to have gotten my wish—a truly spectacular Fourth of July.

Hope you all had a sparkly and safe one.

Love,

Alexa
Aka Trailer Trash

Lewis and Clark Found This Place, and So Did We! Great Falls, MT

We've all heard about the Lewis and Clark Expedition. It's almost as well-known as this pilot and princess venture, but how many of you remember the history behind it all? Just in case you don't, here's a tiny lesson. First of all, put away your high heels if you plan to follow in the footsteps of Lewis and Clark. The scope and adventure of their journey is unmatched in American history and ranks among major explorations of the world. If you prefer to do your exploring in the comfort of your home, you can visit www.lewisandclark bicentennial.com. But first, the president of the United States in 1805 was Thomas Jefferson. He sent Meriwether Lewis & William Clark to find the headwaters of the Missouri River and an inland passageway to the Pacific Ocean. Many people think that the expedition came as a result of the Louisiana Purchase, but Jefferson had it planned before. As a matter of fact, the Purchase was only supposed to include New Orleans, but the diplomats of France, Spain, England, and America got into the act, and the rest is history, plus Creole and beignets. Approximately one quarter of their exploration was what is now within Montana, and you can pretty much follow their route on highways through every region of the state. I'm not going to go into every river, lake, prairie, waterfall, Indian tribe, and mountain range involved. Suffice it to say that it was rough-and-tumble, but only one life was lost, and that was a case of appendicitis. As an aside for the ladies, there was the importance of Sacagawea, the Indian woman who was brought along to help as an interpreter. She was instrumental in successful dealings with Indians en route, and there was only one encounter that resulted in violence. The Indians were friendly and helpful. They guided the expedition and often kept the travelers from starving, and to my mind, got a bad deal from us. Traveling through some of the reservations out there, it appears that they still suffer, but that's for another time.

Although I would love for you all to think I was really smart, much of my information was learned this week at the Lewis and Clark Interpretive Center in Great Falls. It was the brilliant idea and dream of a few history buffs. It was completed in 1998 at a cost of six million dollars. Nearly 80,000 tourists a year visit the 25,000-foot center.

The exhibits are ingenious, educational, interactive, and fun. I wish I had a small child with me because even T-Rex cannot compete with the enthusiasm of the kids I saw going through the place. As a visitor, I was able to mimic the journey, with one side showing what's happening to Lewis and Clark, while the other side explained the culture of the tribes they met or examples of animals and plants they found. Exhibits are hands on, so I smelled some canteen water (yuck), petted an ermine skin, and tested my strength at rope-pulling up a hill. I think this is where the expression "paddling upstream" started. I'm impressed by all of this, as you can tell, and am convinced more than ever that travel is the ultimate learning experience. Hope I'm not boring you with these reports, but you can always scroll down if they are.

Love to you all. The trip is more than half over, and I can't believe how quickly it has gone.

Alexa
Aka Trailer Trash

The sign at the entrance to the interpretive center reminds us that just a handful of dedicated people can make colossal changes in the world. How true!

Gurgle, Drip, Freeze . . . Glacier National Park, and Going-to-the-Sun Road, 2003
St. Mary, Montana

Montana is not a love-at-first-sight experience, especially after coming through Wyoming, which sets the precedent for big and beautiful. Montana is more like true love. After you get to know it, it grows on you, stays with you, and even long after it's out of sight, it remains unforgettable.

Now, let us talk about water. A single drop of water melts from a snowpack, travels several thousand miles, affects lives, and fills many roles. On the way, the water may erode canyons, quench the thirst of a grizzly bear, or provide a home for a mountain trout. It will irrigate crops and generate power. It will find its way into your home or business. It will be heated, cooled, boiled, sprayed, drank, mixed, treated, and probably wasted many times. In the end, it finds the way to one of the oceans, eventually evaporates, and begins the cycle all over again. Look around you right now and try to guess how much water it took to produce the concrete or wood that built your home. Did you know that every car you see took 65,000 gallons to produce, and even your lunch used 1,500 gallons to grow and produce? Why all this about water? Because it is the essence of Glacier National Park, and as the snow melts, streams and waterfalls come to life. Waterton-Glacier is blessed by its location at the "Crown of the Continent" (just about thirty miles from the Canadian border), and the origin of three great river systems: the south Saskatchewan that spills into the Hudson, the Missouri, which flows to the Gulf of Mexico, and the Columbia, which runs into the Pacific. Now we can all go on Jeopardy and win big bucks. But first, the park.

The star attraction of it is called Going-to-the-Sun Road, the historic highway that scales the heights of the Continental Divide at Logan's Pass. We rode in on the bike from the east end. It was windy, cold, and overcast. I had on as many layers as a Martha Stewart wedding cake and still wasn't warm enough. I plugged in my heated vest and hunkered down. We went as far as Logan's Pass, which is about a third of the way in, and then wonder of wonders, even T-Rex, opted to return to town for warm, homemade huckleberry pie and hot coffee. They are pie fanatics around here, and the specialties are huckleberry, blueberry, chokecherry, and raspberry. Very slimming and nutritious, especially when you wear one of the graphic tees that says "Pie is life." Who knew?

The second day we got the award-winning chamber of commerce weather day. The Going-to-the-Sun Road was shining brightly, and we rode the bike all the way through to the other side (approximately fifty miles). It is a narrow and steep road that starts out hugging the wooded shore and then gradually climbs and tunnels through and around the rocky peaks. The views were stirring, and I was so dazzled by the glistening glaciers, mountain goats, and bluer-than-blue lakes that I forgot about the cliffs and drop-offs and just took it all in. Waterfalls, wildflowers, hiking trails, boats, forests, and the smell of pine were everywhere.

I'm vaguely remembering something from the Celestine Prophecy book about trees and why they're so special. Well, in this park, they're absolutely life-giving—and maybe even life-extending. I know it's all that oxygen, but it's something else beyond that. This is a magnificent and special place. The evergreens are dark green and dense. It looks like Christmas in July. It was a glorious day, and nothing short of reconstructive surgery could have wiped the smiles off our faces. All this as a result of a drop of magic water. Think about that the next time you let your faucet keep running.

Thanks for all your emails. I love hearing from you, so keep them coming.

Love,

Alexa
Aka Trailer Trash

Powwows and Snow Cones

We will be leaving Big Sky Country for Idaho today, but who are we kidding? Idaho isn't exactly small potatoes (sorry, I couldn't resist).

Actually, I don't think there is a Western landscape that isn't big and bold and beautiful. On our way, we will be passing through Glacier County, which is so large it is home to an entire nation—the Blackfeet Indians. Since we heard they were having their annual powwow, we decided to stop by Browning, MT, the heart of the reservation and the host city. Unfortunately, Browning is a town that needs an extreme makeover. It reminds me in a way of Belle Glade, FL. It's poor, rundown looking, and loaded with tacky Indian souvenirs. In the midst of all this tackiness, I did manage to find the spectacular Museum of the Plains Indians, which has magnificent Indian paintings, tools, weapons, jewelry, ceremonial gear, and clothing. But fry bread and "Made in China" moccasins were in greater supply.

The word *powwow* originally referred to the spiritual men and medicine men of the tribe, but the Americans misunderstood it to mean the entire tribe, and that definition stuck.

Now, about the powwow! It looked more like a state fair with T-shirts and snow cones and even plastic the Hulk balloons for sale. We entered a makeshift arena with dirt floors and bleacher seating. And then the opening ceremonies began—a color guard with flag bearers from the US and Canadian military, plus some POWs and Indian chiefs wearing feather headdresses that trailed behind them in fluffy splendor. They were all on foot, silent at first, and then hundreds of Blackfeet Indians wearing full ceremonial garb followed in a primitive procession. There is not any painting I have ever seen of Indians that could begin to capture this sight. The bright colors—red, yellow, turquoise—the animal skins that were made into dresses and pants, the intricate beading of roses, eagles, snakes, and all kinds of symbolic figures, fringes, bells, and a variety of ornate and elaborate decorations.

Some were carrying tomahawks with beaded handles. Some had faces painted, emphasizing cheekbones that rivaled Garbo's. All were solemn-faced. The drumming began, and then the chanting, and then the dancing. It was a hesitant double-step with an occasional whirling and dipping, especially beautiful when the headdresses tossed and lifted with the movements.

This was a competition for the best traditional outfit, handmade by wives, ex-wives, mothers, men, and the children. As the drumming and chanting continued, we were mesmerized by the beauty and dignity of this group. Just for a moment, we were transported back to a time when the Blackfeet controlled the buffalo county east of the mountains. The moment passed, and we were drummed out to the concession area. We got snow cones and some fry bread and hoped that our photographs might do justice to a people who have not seen a lot of justice in our country.

Love to you all. Idaho is next.

Alexa
Aka Trailer Trash

Coeur d'Alene, Seaplanes, and the 14th Hole
2003

On the road to Coeur d'Alene, Idaho, from Montana, you "can't see the forest for the trees." (A Renaissance proverb written by John Heywood in 1546). There are wall-to-wall evergreens on both sides and no billboards to interrupt the green highway. Just like I-95, right? Now, let's think about Idaho.

Aside from the potato and the fact that this state is wedged between Washington and Oregon, most everything else about it is unknown to most people, and that includes me. Even Ernest Hemingway, who wrote part of *For Whom the Bell Tolls* in a room at Sun Valley, thought he didn't know a lot about Idaho.

Well, part of that was because he probably didn't leave his room very often. Whether because of this or in spite of it, Ernest ended up liking the state so much that he enjoyed his passions of hunting and fishing here and spent his last days in Ketchum, his final resting place. At any rate, Idaho is something of an enigma.

Coeur d'Alene was a complete surprise in the middle of all this Western atmosphere—a true resort town with all the polish and refinement that Miami Beach should have. The centerpiece of the town is an enormous sapphire blue lake that sits and sparkles against the green landscape. Seeing this, I can understand why Idaho is called "The Gem State." But the real reason is because they mine silver and other metals there, but I like my reason better.

The most recognizable landmark is a high-rise hotel that towers (elegantly) over the lakefront above a three-quarter-mile floating boardwalk. Therefore, everyone walks on water, in a manner of speaking. The other claim to fame here—attention, all golfers—is the only floating golf green on the planet. If you're accurate enough to get your ball onto the fourteenth hole, a little speedboat runs you out to the green to putt. I've never seen anything like it. The driving range is also waterfront, and of course, the balls float. This is all part of a five-star resort complex, and in my opinion, worth a special trip to experience it.

The origin of the name Coeur d'Alene is subject to debate, but in French it means "heart of awl," and it's also the name of a now defunct Indian tribe. That's "awl" I know. The Indians still own a lot of land around here, and we see many casinos as we pass through the little towns. Haven't been inside any of them. I'm not much of a gambler when it comes to money, plus, I'd rather be outdoors.

We toured the lake on a double-decker boat, with the captain giving us points of interest over the loudspeaker. It's touristy, but so much fun, and we talked to lots of people from all over the USA. Most of them wore sandals with socks. We were totally impressed with the size of the lake, the marinas, the expensive homes, and the restaurants, and everything is immaculate. No garbage. Not even a cigarette butt.

Then we took to the air. It was my first ride in a seaplane, and we swooped over and around the beautiful lake. We had to dodge parasails, helicopters, and ospreys, but what a view! I was a little reluctant to go because our pilot was at least eighty and practically deaf, but he gave us a great ride, and besides, I knew Craig could take over if anything happened. It's really nice to travel with your own pilot.

We took the motorcycle over to the next town of Sandpoint, which, among other things, has the first original Coldwater Creek store. (My catalog junkie friends will recognize that name.) It's also near Ruby Ridge. You may recall the ugly shooting incident that happened there between the FBI and the Weaver family. At the time, it was on the news every day.

Summing up, I'd have to say that there is a simple, rugged individualist character here that feeds the popular notion that Idaho is the last true vestige of the Western frontier. I don't know if that's true, but I do know it's almost impossible to get an Idaho potato around here.

Love to you all.

Alexa
Aka Trailer Trash

We're zigzagging back to Missoula, MT. Just saw a bumper sticker that said "Keep honkin', I'm reloading."

Moose Drool and Music

We're in Missoula, MT. Why would anyone come here? Well, because it's an artsy and outdoorsy place, a hip big/little town with a Western twang, lots of restaurants, galleries, and one-of-a-kind shops, plus the University of Montana. But none of those things are why I wanted to come here. The main attraction for me is a dark chocolate brown ale called Moose Drool that I discovered last year in Montana. Unfortunately, the drool is only available in Montana, Idaho, Wyoming, and maybe a couple of other places in the northwest. Its maker, the Big Sky Brewing Company is here, and I was hoping for a tour, a tasting, and a way to ship some to Miami and to Jeremy in NYC. Well, two out of three ain't bad. No tour, and no shipping unless you pack it and wrap it yourself and then take it to a private post office. We ended up doing that furtively. I felt like James Bond, and this will forever be known as the "drool scam." We did get to taste lots of drool and bought some very funny caps, tees, and mugs. By the way, some of the beers here have really unusual names: Skydiver Blonde, Slow Elk, Pikes Kilt Lifter, Scape Goat, Trout Slayer, Bitch Creek, and Buckin' Horse, to name a few. I think the makers have been drinking a lot of their own stuff to come up with these.

Full of drool, we were able to attend the seventh annual International Choral Festival held at the University of Montana. You can imagine how thrilled T-Rex was at the thought of sitting through several classical selections. If that wasn't bad enough, the air-conditioning was turned off because they claimed it would interfere with the recording quality. We think that sweating also has negative effects. I loved it. He tolerated it. These are world-class groups that have all recorded and performed all over the world. Our performance included the Greensboro Youth Chorus, the Coro Femenino de la Pontifica from Peru, and Coceval, an all-male choir from Angola. These concerts go on all weekend and are free to the public. They are privately funded, and the citizens of Missoula house all the participants. I was so glad to have had this opportunity. A truly elevating event.

Love to you all.

Alexa
Aka Trailer Trash

P.S. I'm told that beer isn't just for breakfast anymore.

Smoke Jumpers

What if we were going back to school in the fall and were called on to report, "What did you do this summer?" Just imagine past the family trips to Disney World and dude ranches, summer jobs, sleep-away camps, spa vacations, and golfing weekends. But what if you were a smoke jumper? We toured the headquarters for these incredible firefighters in Missoula, MT. I'm sure you've read about them. They are the highly trained specialists who parachute from planes (old DC-3s) into remote areas of national forests to fight wildfires. Typical profile of a smoke jumper: between 5'6" and 6'2", weighs between 115 and 200 pounds, not older to start than fifty. Fifty-seven is retirement age. They are required to work out ninety minutes every day (well, that eliminates the majority of us right there). Their real jobs (they do this just for summer fun) are schoolteachers, ski patrollers, and ski instructors. They earn $13.00 an hour. They are mostly men, but there are a few women. The gear they jump with weighs ninety-five pounds. The gear includes food, first aid, books, and maps. They wear Kevlar jumpsuits inspired by Elvis (no kidding) and motorcycle helmets with a face mask. The most common injury is an ankle sprain, and they're all crazy.

FYI, I scanned the list of jumper names in search of a Goldstein or Schwartz, but there were none. No self-respecting Jewish mother would allow her son to jump out of a plane and into a forest fire. They jump from 1,500 feet (takes about ninety seconds), about 1.5 miles away from the fires, and hike in wearing all that gear. Oy! Such a schlep!

The food they eat includes dehydrated tiramisu, Emergen-C — "the champagne of nutritional drinks"—and a big favorite, foil-wrapped Spam, which they sprinkle with dried Gatorade and then fry. Do you think Emeril is in on this? At any rate, I hope there's some Alka Seltzer in the drop pack. We toured the inspection room, which looks like a scene from the movie *Coma*. Just-used parachutes are hanging from ceiling hooks and are assessed for replacement, cleaning, or repair. Riggers do the repairs and packing, and all the SJs are expected to learn to use sewing machines and repair some of their own rips. It takes approximately forty-five minutes to pack a chute, and no one is allowed to pack for anyone else until they have successfully packed twenty chutes. I bet they know how to fold a fitted bottom sheet. They work a maximum of twenty-one days before they have a day off and are on call. It's starting to sound like a doctor with a death wish.

Smoke jumpers started in 1939, and there are three hundred of them. This summer, the West has been besieged with fires, and these guys are out there nonstop. I admire their courage, their fitness, and their sense of humor. A big sign in the locker room reads: "Stupid hurts." These summertime heroes are an eclectic group. Some of them do it for the glory, but most do it because they think it needs to be done, and it's a thrill they get paid for. Some of them are quiet, some are pranksters. All of them are fearless, and I even found a book of poetry as thick as the Miami phonebook full of the rhymes and free verses written by smoke jumpers.

I was so impressed with all this, I suited up in my pj's, jumped right onto the Airstream couch, and tore into true survival food: Double Stuf Oreos. T-Rex had already eaten the Spam.

Love to you all.

Alexa
Aka Trailer Trash

Trivia From the Road

Have you ever tried "swingin' steak"? Well, it's not a perverted bull, but rather sliced and crisped bull testicles, served with cocktail sauce (is this a play on words?) and lemon wedges. How many cosmos would I have to drink before I ate all that? And speaking of picky eaters, for those of my friends who have witnessed me time and time and time again say no to salmon, out here, the Pacific salmon is delicious—no fishy, salmony taste at all.

Here are a few incidents, things, and signs I've seen that I thought were worth sharing: An "I showered at the Bates Motel" T-shirt at the Bates Motel in Idaho. We all know that this isn't the real one because that was filmed in California, but the creepy owner has really capitalized on the name, and I was devastated to find out he had just sold the last of the shirts to a group of bikers. I will try their website Batesmotel@adelphia.net when I return.

"Please buy something here. My grandson needs a canoe." This is a sign in front of a general store in Lolo Pass, MT. "Unattended children will be eaten by grizzlies" is the sign at a hot springs swimming pool in Montana. "Thou shalt not park in the blue space or thou shalt be towed" is the sign in the parking lot of the Lutheran church in Missoula, MT.

A beautiful woman—with her family—who was parked next to us at a KOA, asked one of the toughest questions on the trip: "Do you know God?"

This question didn't come as a complete surprise because we had been inside her trailer, and it was pretty obvious from all the photos of Jesus and crucifixes on the wall that she was a born-again Christian. I didn't think this was a trick question, but I had no immediate answer for fear that our Airstream would be struck down if I answered incorrectly. Please send any suggested answers because I have a feeling this will happen again.

The F-15 pilot, now a retired Lt. Colonel, and his wife also had an Airstream. They were in the same RV park as we were in Idaho. He said this was his second Airstream in two years. When I asked him how come, he said, "I rolled the first one." I thought it was ironic that he who should be so incredibly skilled in the sky flipped a practically unflippable trailer. Oh well. I guess he's used to being upside down. Pretty scary stuff!

And last but not least, a true story told to me by my first cousin, Ann, who lives with Susan, her life partner of twenty-two years, in Eugene, Oregon, where we are right now. Ann is a registered nurse, and she was working in a small hospital in town, waiting patiently at a clerk's desk to sign something. A woman came up to the desk and noticed Ann's necklace. It was a gold Star of David welded inside the circle of her mother's wedding ring. The woman asked Ann, "Is that a Star of David?" Ann said, "Yes, it is." The woman made a disgusted face, harrumphed, and walked back to where she was sitting with someone in the waiting room. Ann overheard her say, "I'm glad we don't have more of those people around." Ann was so stunned by this remark that she said nothing. Contemplating the episode later, here's what she wished she had said: "And if you think that's bad, I'm a lesbian, too."

Also, I have concluded that Cracker Barrel is the number-one franchise we have found on the road. Did I tell you this already? Here's why: location, location, location. They are always right on or off the highway exits and have big recognizable signs. They provide brain teaser games at the dining tables. (You know, leave the least number of pegs in the holes and prove you're not really a moron.) The food, although not fabulous, is consistent, especially the breakfasts. The wait staff is always friendly and cheerful. They have skim milk (a rarity on the road). They have shopping, including cute gifts, games, and Katherine's phenomenal chocolate chip cookies in the blue and white package. They rent books on tape, which you can turn in at the next Cracker Barrel you visit. They have rocking chairs on the porch. They sell *USA Today*, our touchstone to the real world. They have fireplaces, not a big plus in Florida, but elsewhere. They provide goat milk hand cream in the bathroom, which is very silky, and the biscuits and honey are really good.

That's all for now. Love and kisses.

Alexa
Aka Trailer Trash

Sun Valley — "Roses and Lollipops"

We're on the road to Sun Valley, Idaho, along the Salmon River Scenic Byway. I was expecting the little pink guys to be posing for us and flashing their fins, but they were probably too hot. It's so hot that I'm sure the fish would grill themselves on the pavement if they chose to flip out and try to hitch a ride. No takers so far, but I learned a new word—*anadromous*, as in fish that start out life in fresh water, mature in the saltwater ocean, and then return to fresh water at the end of life. In case you haven't guessed, this applies to salmon.

This part of the West is full of hot mineral springs, so we decided to partake in the waters at Challis (pronounced chalice). Ten minutes in 106 degrees of minerals is supposed to do wonders. We'll see, but personally, I think old-fashioned Epson Salts work as well. Now on to the glamorous valley!

My first trip to Sun Valley was sometime in the late 1970s with the Miami Ski Club, and my memories are vague but very sentimental. That story for another time, perhaps.

When Union Pacific executive Averell Harriman sent his expert scout count, Felix Schaff Gotsch, out West to find the ideal location for a European–style ski resort, he struck gold.

The special charm still holds, even in summertime, and especially at the Sun Valley Lodge. This is an old-world Ritz Carlton type of place with swans in the lake, sleigh rides/hay rides, trap and skeet shooting, ice shows, tennis, golf, bowling, and a formal dining room featuring French cuisine. Also, the world's first chairlift was built there. We stayed in an RV park in Ketchum, which is only a mile away. For those of you who are still under the misconception that staying in a mobile home is only for Trailer Trash, I have yet another example to the contraire, and *he* was in our RV park. If any of you out there graduated high school with me, you may or may not remember senior prom. For me, it's also a vague memory, but I do remember the theme. It was "Roses and Lollipops" from the song by Jack Jones. For those of you who dare to be younger than me or weren't into easy-listening, Jack Jones was the handsome crooner who sang "The Impossible Dream" and "Call Me Irresponsible" and performed at the Diplomat Hotel in the Tack Room and big night club rooms. I saw him there a long time ago, and now forty years later, he was in a motorcoach, just a stanza space away. Did I meet him? Yes. Was he charming? Yes. He came over to the Airstream and visited with us one evening. We even exchanged phone numbers. I'm not waiting by the phone, but it was a real thrill to connect the person with some of my favorite songs. I'll let you know if he calls.

I have a fun friend who spends her summers in Sun Valley, and we went to her country club, saw her gorgeous house, and met some of the summer crowd. It may surprise you to know that we held our own amidst the chatter about "pheasie" hunting, racehorses, and yes, private jets. All the ladies wanted to go for motorcycle rides by the time T-Rex got through with them. I think it's the leather thing!

Then, after studying the map (I'm doing much better), I decided that it wasn't all that far to go to Eugene, Oregon, next (only a day or so drive) and visit my cousin Ann. After all, when am I ever going to be this close again? Plus, it's a perfect opportunity to listen nonstop to the Jack Jones CD I just bought. "Hello, Ann. Guess who's coming to dinner?"

Love to you all.

Alexa
Aka Trailer Trash

Idaho, the Schlep State

All our states have special descriptive names that are supposed to describe their resources, commerce, or terrain. For example, Florida, the Sunshine State; Missouri, the Show Me State; Washington, the Evergreen State; and New York, the Empire State. Idaho is called "The Gem State" and has over eighty varieties of sparkly things within its borders. That being named, I have a new nickname for Idaho—the Schlep State! First of all, it's a lot easier to schlep with a truck, and here, the trucks outnumber the cars. I could count on one hand the number of BMWs, Porsches, and Mercedes I've seen. Next, in addition to four-wheel drive and snow chains, every truck comes fully equipped with a dog. I'm not sure if you get to pick the breed, color, or size, but there is always one, ears and fur flying in the breeze when you drive off the dealer's lot.

There also must be an unwritten state law that requires every vehicle to tow or carry something. We've seen it all: canoes, rafts, totem poles, tents, fishing gear, antiques, potatoes, motorcycles, log homes, double-wide homes, children, pigs, horses, and even an airplane (with the wings off and strapped on top). The bungee cord business here must be phenomenal.

With all the forests, mountain lakes, mountains, ore hounds, and campers in pursuit of their pastimes, it's a wonder that the highways aren't overcrowded. But no, we can cruise along and sometimes never see another vehicle for miles, but when we do, it's always schlepping something. Ironically, most of the people in Idaho have never heard of the word, but I think they invented it.

Love, and happy schlepping.

Alexa
Aka Trailer Trash

Eugene, Oregon . . . Worth the Drive
2003

We traveled through the high desert from Sun Valley on the way to Eugene, Oregon (pronounce it Ore'gun, or else you will be corrected). The high temperature was hovering between 112 and 116 degrees. We were elated when it went below 100 at about 5:00 p.m. Finally, we arrived at the delightful town called Sisters. It's named for three of the Cascade Mountains—Faith, Hope, and Charity—and this is a town that knows how to sell itself. Main Street has been completely rebuilt after a fire destroyed it, but it maintains an old and friendly appearance. We missed the annual quilt show, during which the entire town is strung with all kinds of patterns, shapes, and sizes. The locals told me it was a real artistic show hung from clotheslines in front of every store. I was also told about a fabulous week that invites real sisters or just great friends to participate in a variety of girly-girl/women things: makeovers, yoga, book reviews, spa treatments, hiking, biking, rafting treks, and lectures on all the topics we like. Gather 'round, sistas!

But I'm heading this way to see my first cousin, Ann. She and her life partner, Susan, were waiting for us and showed us as much as they could in three days. On one of the days, they took us to the ruggedly beautiful Pacific Coast. So, my question to you is, if you're blindfolded, how do you tell the difference between the Atlantic and Pacific oceans? Here's how! The Pacific is windy. The Pacific is really windy. The Pacific is hold-on-to-your-head-and-the-person-you're-with windy. You'll hear the crashing of waves and maybe the barking of sea lions. Or just cut to the chase, put your toe in the water, and turn blue within sixty seconds. Now, if you take off your blindfolds, you will see few swimmers. Also, swimmers have very white skin, wear wet suits, not thongs, and have signed their life insurance policies. Next, the sand is a honey beige, and the water looks as if navy blue marbles are rolling in it. There are cliffs surrounding the beaches and smooth, blue-grey rocks on the beach. There are no high-rises lining the shore, and sand dunes are the size of Costco.

It was definitely one of the windiest days on the coast, but we just had to go on a group dune buggy safari. My hooded sweatshirt and lined leather jacket were *almost* enough to keep me from the chill, but I did enjoy the free microdermabrasion treatment from the blowing sand. Our dune buggy was a converted old topless school bus, with cage-like roll bars. You mean, we can turn over? We lumbered along the beaches, up 100-foot-high sand hills, and then careened down them like a roller coaster. I would've smiled more, or maybe even screamed, but sand is so tough to get out of your teeth. But I would love to go again.

Eugene is the hazelnut capital of the US and one of the only cities I've visited where I picked wild blackberries in the streets.

And in case you've ever wondered where all the hippies have gone, check out Eugene's Saturday open market. The favorite T-shirt slogan there is "We're here because we're not all here." But they are all there: dream interpreters, healers, juicers, origami artists, glass blowers, beading beatniks, and tie-dyed everything. I wanted to hand out free razors to the women, but I resisted.

Visiting with my cousin was wonderful. She and Susan have a pretty house, two precious fluffy white dogs, good jobs, and friends. Ann was walking in a relay for a life event, and we accompanied her for a lap or two. The entire community seemed to be part of this, and it was a real happening. She walked from 7:00 p.m. until 8:00 the next morning. The concept is that cancer never rests, so the walkers don't either. There were rock bands, food, people hanging out in tents, and luminaires (did I make up this word?) honoring loved ones lining the track.

We accidentally met another celebrity—surfer dude and entrepreneur, Ron Jon. I've seen his billboards all over Florida highways for years, and there he was in Eugene, taking delivery of his million-dollar Prevost/Featherlight motorcoach. It caught our eyes in the parking lot at the dealership, and we just had to stop and gawk at the unbelievable paint job. From a distance, it looked like a real Woody (a huge one) with paneling, but up close, they were just the best graphics I've ever seen. He's Australian and looks like a taller Crocodile Dundee. His wife Lynn invited me inside their coach to look at the interior (woman to woman), and I must say carpeting sculpted to look like a wave might be the next new design trend. They were as nice as could be, and when I told them Jeremy was having his first surfing experience at that moment, they gave me some discount coupons and stickers for him. By the way, Jeremy hung ten the first time, which his teacher said was "Awesome, dude!"

Time to kiss my cousins goodbye. We leave with lots of great memories and have possibly accelerated their interest in Trailer Trash travel. There could be more Airstreamers in the family soon. We'll be heading east tomorrow if we can get past all the cute little espresso drive-throughs. It's no wonder Starbucks got its start out this way. These people are total caffeine freaks. Miami ought to have mini, fresh-squeezed orange juice drive-throughs, too. Help me think up some cool names for these juicy vitamin C gems. It could be the start of the big bucks, and healthy, too. How about "Orange you glad you live in Florida"?

Love to you all.

Alexa
Aka Trailer Trash

And a River Runs Through It— The Northwest Passage
Sunday, July 27

We drove along the massive Columbia River on the way out of Oregon and briefly touched Washington state. This is once again the Lewis and Clark Trail, and I cannot imagine their exuberance upon discovering this watery passage to the Pacific. This is a true gateway to the world, and we sighted barges loaded with containers being pushed and pulled by the mules of the river—the tugboats. Huge dams control the flow of water and boating traffic of all kinds. My favorites are the classic Chris Craft open speedboats made of solid mahogany, usually sporting an American flag fluttering from the stern. Classic vintage!

On into Walla Walla and the Yakima Valley, which boast the highest number of fruit trees anywhere in the USA. I'm having fresh huckleberries with lunch, and probably for dinner, too. And then we sip with the snake!

On the hilly mounds alongside the Snake River, conditions are ideal for growing grapes. The Walla and Yakima Valley areas are part of the Columbia Valley. We've read that this area wins more awards proportional to production than any other region in the world. We noted several small, unostentatious vineyards everywhere. Unfortunately, it was after hours, and we were unable to sample any wine, but I will definitely look into Washington state brands when I stock up next at home. We spent the night in Clarkston at the mouth of Hells Canyon. At 5,500 feet, it's the deepest river gorge in the US. The jetboat rides through the canyon look awesome.

And now for my epiphany! We detoured around the town of Walla Walla because a bridge was being repaired, and we ended up in the middle of hundreds of acres of wheat farmland and giant granaries. It was just before dusk, and the sinking sun was casting that magic shadow light that photographers always talk about in California. But it didn't look like anything we had seen before—a soft honey color covered the vast glowing fields. The freshly mowed rows of grain looked like unfurled banners blowing in the wind. There was the feeling of the hills moving, but there was no breeze.

"What is this?" I asked.

T-Rex was silent (not unusual). Ten minutes later, I got my answer. (Not from him.) The honey color is amber. The banners are waves. We were right smack in the middle of "America the Beautiful," and the fields of grain that look like waves. Imagine all those times I've sung or heard the song but never really understood the visual impact this sight must have had on the composer. It's an indescribable feeling to see something like this. And that makes nine hours in the truck worth it. This time, I resisted singing.

Hoping to see the splendor of some purple mountains next.

Love to you all.

Alexa
Aka Trailer Trash

Who is Bob Witson?
Deer Lodge, MT
July 2003

For the past twenty-six years, Bob Witson's best colors have been black and white. His best views have been through steel bars, and his best companion has been himself. Witson is currently serving a double life sentence in Montana State Prison because he was an accomplice to a murder in 1976. He has been turned down for parole twice, as recently as three months ago. He is a Texan who didn't have a high school GED or a trade. He is at once an ordinary and unusual man, and now I'll tell you why and how we met him.

We were traveling in Deer Lodge, MT, and toured the old Montana prison, the pioneer museum, and the antique auto museum. The old prison was opened before Montana even became a state. A member of the Butch Cassidy gang was incarcerated there, and some really rough characters of the Old West were, as well. (Some women, too.) I've never been in a prison before, and this one, built by the inmates, looks like a medieval fortress with turret towers for guardhouses. It's a grim and foreboding four-story, brick-and-stone building with tunnels, holding cells, gunports, and barbed wire. In 1959, a prison riot necessitated bringing in the National Guard, and the damage done to the towers with their bazookas is still visible. This was not a nice place to live, and I felt a heaviness as I walked through the dark and damp narrow spaces, imagining the sordid and solitary existence within these walls.

Oxygen. I felt like I needed oxygen! But there was an unexpected breath of fresh air at the end of the tunnels and just outside the walls.

Bob Witson was an inmate in the old prison for sixteen months before being moved to the new state prison. A couple of years ago, a Montana state official (I don't know his exact title) decided to open a prison retail gift shop right across the street from the old prison. It has become quite a tourist attraction, with many daily visitors. The store sells artwork made by the prisoners, and they receive eighty percent of the proceeds if a piece of their work sells. This money goes toward lowering their debts, child support, etc. We ambled in to have a look. Some of the items were beaded belts, horsehair bridals, tooled leather wallets and handbags, jewelry, and paintings. All handmade. I'm not sure if I was more impressed with the workmanship or surprised by the unique concept. Certainly, I was astounded that so many beautifully crafted items had been created in an environment that I had felt suffocated in after only a few minutes. I've shopped all over the world, but to my knowledge, this is the only store of its kind. I wondered, how could such beautiful things be created in such a dark fortress? Is this a striking example of the human spirit rising above adversity? Or is it just something the inmates do to pass the time?

Who is Bob Witson? Well, he is still a prisoner, but he is also the unlikely manager of the shop. He's dropped off every morning and picked up every afternoon when he returns to his quarters. He handles thousands of dollars in cash (they don't take credit cards). He is unsupervised. He deals with the public and is three feet from the wide-open door all day. He has a phone, but it only calls the prison.

We came into the shop just to look, not knowing any of this. We said hello and told him we had just visited the old prison, and that's when he said he had spent sixteen months there . . . and then the rest of his story came rambling out. At first, we were fascinated by this 50-ish, soft-spoken man. After all, it was a novelty for me to talk to someone serving two life sentences because he was an accomplice to murder. But the novelty quickly wore off, and we really took a liking to him. He didn't seem to mind my many questions.

The first one was, "How did you get this job?"

According to Witson, after the state decided to open the store, they also decided they wanted it run by an inmate. Out of thirteen hundred men, only five qualified, and out of the five, Bob Witson was chosen. From the start, he was an exemplary prisoner. One who knew how to set boundaries from the bullies. One who self-educated with correspondence courses. And one who had an art that he worked at diligently. Wood carving. After a half an hour's conversation, I asked him an unthinkable question. Did he feel he had been unjustly sentenced? His reply was, "No, miss. I stood by and let it happen."

We spoke some more, and he admitted he was absolutely terrified on his first days in the store. He told us he had no social skills, no ability to talk to people, and was intimidated by the outside world, which had changed a lot in a quarter of a century. He told us he laughed when he looked at money for the first time. "All those big picture faces."

It's almost a year since he started his job, which he now loves. And he has made the adjustment. The people of Deer Lodge really like him. They come by to visit and bring him cookies and treats. When I spoke with the man—who owned the business next door—about him, he said he'd hire him in a minute, when and if he gets out.

And then I shopped. I bought several gifts for friends and family, each one made by a different inmate, and with every gift I gave, I told the story of Bob Witson. I've never felt better about spending money than I did in that store, knowing that each purchase, no matter how small, was going to make a difference to a whole lot of people a lot less fortunate than I am. Obviously, Bob Witson is an exception—one out of 1,300—but I applaud the state of Montana. With all its casinos, they've taken a real gamble on a convict. If I were a betting woman, I'd bet that next year, Bob Witson will still be there, three feet from an open door. And if I'm wrong, then we all lose the bet.

Love to you all, and cherish your freedom.

Alexa
Aka Trailer Trash

P.S. This just overheard in Bowman, MT: "How are you? Well, I'm just as fine as frog hairs."

Vroom, Vroom, Vroom
August 1–6, Bike Week Sturgis, South Dakota

Once a year, this town is transformed from almost nothing into motorcycle mayhem. It hasn't rained in South Dakota in weeks, but the sound of thunder is everywhere. It's the biggest bike rally in America, and an estimated 500,000 motorcycles are here. Even though the rally was started years ago by a guy who had an Indian brand motorcycle, 498,000 of the ones here are Harley Davidsons. One of their best-known slogans is "loud pipes save lives," and as a result of that, there is going to be an entire generation of senior bikers who are alive but deaf. In the meantime, I'm wearing earplugs! It's at times like this that I wish I could swap my ears for an extra pair of eyes. I can barely take it all in—the scenery, the bikers, plus all the wonderful things to do here. I really hope that none of *Vogue*'s fashionistas plan on featuring fringe or black leather this year, because every last scrap of it is here. Even the cows I've seen lately are brown and happy about it.

So, what are they like, these bikers? Well, if you can get past the beards, the ponytails, the lace, the tattoos, the thongs, the bare chests, the chaps with nothing on under them, the silver chains, the beer bellies, and the doo-rags (cotton bandanas tightly wrapped on the head instead of helmets), the deer antlers on helmets, guys on mopeds juggling beer cans, and the women who will show their "mommy parts" for a twenty-five-cent strand of colored beads, I guess they are a mixed bag. Some are lawyers, doctors, and artists, but it's hard to tell because even though they're friendly and polite, none of them want to talk about anything besides exhausts and chrome.

And, despite the idolized rugged individual image, a la James Dean and Marlon Brando, they all wear the same unofficial uniform: blue denims and black T-shirts. They ride in packs, and they party in groups.

*T-Rex and I are as big a novelty here as a vegan in a steakhouse. We're riding a quiet BMW. We ride alone. We always wear our helmets and some sort of protective gear (that's for you, Mom).

The Harley riders are somewhat fascinated with us. When our bike is parked, we've seen a couple of guys get down on the ground and look underneath Craig's bike. As a career pilot, Craig values performance and reliability. Harleys have a reputation for breaking down, and we see them doing just that, daily, on the sides of the roads.

And then there's our shiny little Airstream trailer. In an area with thousands of people camping out in motor homes, trailers, tents, and sleeping bags, we may have the only Airstream trailer in Sturgis. Turns out, we're traveling with an American icon, and we didn't know it. We've had some knocks on the door from people who have heard of them all their lives and are just dying to have a look. Go figure! Of course, we let them in. Craig is always carrying . . .

The real question is, what motivates 500,000-plus people to come to Sturgis, SD, for ten days, from all parts of the country and Europe? I'm guessing it's a primal urge. It's male and female bonding. It's leaving all responsibilities behind. It's getting away from stress, traffic, and the civilization we've created. It's men and women roaring around the Black Hills on powerful iron horses. It's the last chance to be cowboys and cowgirls. It's the way we were meant to be—free to roam and explore. It's why we travel, why we venture down *The Road Less Traveled* (a book by Scott Peck). Just a reminder . . . I'm not a real biker. Just a passenger. In fact, I've spent more time on the back of a motorcycle than a pilot fish does on a shark. I've had lots of time back there to think about why I love it and have no fear of it. I guess it all goes back to my childhood. Doesn't everything?

Although there were no motorcycles in our garage, lots of my weekends were spent on the flying bridge of a 34-foot sport fisherman boat with my father at the helm. I could sit happily all day on the bow of his custom-made wave rider, wind in my face, bouncing over the waves, soaking up the sun and the wide-open spaces of Biscayne Bay and the ocean. I remember thinking I was a lucky little girl and that this was the very best place to be. Being with my father always made me feel safe and adventurous. That, and our bareboat family excursions to the Florida Keys and The Bahamas may have primed me for these summer explorations. So, here I am with T-Rex at the wheel, the wind in my face, and an endless horizon of Black Hills. It just feels right. Once again, I feel like a lucky girl, and there is a bonus. You never get seasick on the back of a motorcycle.

Love to you all. Home on the night of August 6th.

Alexa
Aka Trailer Trash

*P.S. T-Rex is my nickname for Craig, a man who can sleep anywhere, eat anything, fix anything, never gets lost, and occasionally roars.

P.P.S. Wait 'til you see my beads!

Love Affairs, and What I Learned on the Road

Somewhere between the road love of Jack Kerouac, E.B. White (he drove cross-country in his Model T in 1922), and Mario Andretti, I figured out that Americans have an ongoing love affair with the open road and anything on two or more wheels. There was even a TV documentary airing on October 6th about the road trip of Horatio Nelson Jackson, who in 1903 spent $8,000 to win a $50 bet that said he couldn't drive from San Francisco to New York in ninety days. He did it in '63. If he had been traveling with T-Rex, he would've done it in a week.

And just think about how many times you've said or heard someone else say, "Someday, I'm going to leave all this behind and hit the road." I don't know what "all this" is for those folks, but getting away from palmetto bugs and voicemail is a good start for me.

I'm home now, or at least the physical part of me is home. My mind hasn't quite adjusted to the kinetic convolutions of city life, phones ringing, security guard gates, appointment books, answering machines, and the overabundance of people. But it's time to review my summer love affair with the road and what I learned out there.

Here's what I learned:

American history

American geography

To look at beautiful things and not have to acquire them.

To be a better map reader.

To live in the moment and not worry about where I'm spending the night.

That less makeup is more attractive, especially if you're smiling.

People are people.

Why fly swatters work.

That Walmart has organic fruits and vegetables.

That men are naturally better at some things.

That there are very few people I could stay in a trailer with for two months.

That the American Indians got a raw deal.

That music makes anything better or bearable for me, i.e., satellite radio is a must for road trips.

That Snapple drink bottle caps have trivia questions.

That Bo Diddley still performs.

That a mountain drop is an outdoor toilet (don't be standing under any cliffs).

That you can get sunburned through a rolled-up truck window.

That status is universal—it's the symbols that are different.

That women need privacy in the bathroom, and men don't care.

I've learned that I don't have to be right all the time, but once every two months would be nice.

I've learned that T-Rex thinks he has nothing left to learn.

I've learned I can get ready in five minutes if it's something I want to do.

I don't mind not driving. (I was a complete non-driver for 8,000 miles.)

I've learned that I have a real attraction to the road—the black taffeta pavement with the cheerful yellow or white line pointing the way . . . away.

I learned that I have a lot more to learn.

I learned that I traveled with a very special person: enthusiastic, generous, friendly, unspoiled, considerate, capable, fun-loving, self-reliant, spontaneous, good-natured, and compromising. Someone who can eat anything and never get a stomachache, can sleep anywhere and never complain, who can make the best of any situation, including flat tires and my moods, and who told me every day how glad he was to have me with him. I was glad, too. Thank you, Craig, for making this all possible.

Love to you all. See you after Labor Day!

Alexa
Aka Trailer Trash

P.S. These are quotes from a Texas woman who sat next to me on the plane from Rapid City to Denver. It was only a 45-minute flight, or I'm sure there would have been more. She was a real pistol!

"Ostriches are so dumb (she raised them in Amarillo) that they stand out in the rain, put their heads up, and take so much water into their lungs that they drown."

Her husband was "as useless as tits on a boar hog." Re: his mechanical abilities.

The definition of "hall fu**ing-passing" each other in the hall and saying "F— you." (They are no longer married)

2004

The Passenger Seat

Well, here I go again, third time's the charm.
Ready for anything, no cause for alarm.
Packed and prepared, getting out of the heat.
I'm sitting sweetly in the passenger seat.

Now the tires could go flat and the fish fail to bite.
Or we could get stuck in the middle of the night.
But I'm playin' my music and putting up my feet.
'Cause I'm sitting sweetly in the passenger seat.

I don't plan to drive this gigantic rig.
It's fifty feet long, shiny, and big.
But in case I do so and it's a disaster,
I'll be coming home alone, and helluva lot faster.

The pilot's in command, he never gets lost.
The princess is letting him be the big boss.
He's got a built-in GPS, and that's pretty neat.
'Cause I'm lost in thought in the passenger's seat.

With T-Rex on my left, the whole country ahead.
A jar of peanut butter will keep us well fed.
No telling where we'll go or who we might meet.
I'll write to you all from the passenger seat.

* * *

Love to you all.

Alexa
Aka Trailer Trash . . . the poet.
Yes, I wrote this.

Sunday, Father's Day
Kitschy Kitschy Coo . . .

It's one of Central Florida's last roadside attractions, and on Father's Day at Weeki Wachee Springs, fathers get in for free when accompanied by their child. Not one to pass up a bargain opportunity, Craig found the youngest ticket-seller, blocked her view of me, and became daddy dearest for the next few hours. Playing the role of the child, I sucked my thumb occasionally and asked to go to the bathroom as often as possible.

Now, for a little story . . . Once upon a time, long, long ago, King Neptune had a beautiful daughter, the little mermaid. Like all fathers, especially Jewish and Italian ones, he wanted her to have a better life, beyond seasickness and touchy-feely sailors. So, he sent her to a fun and tranquil place with lots of daddies. Tada! Weekee Wachee Springs.

It's the only place I know where you can meet a real live mermaid. There were two mermaid shows today, and I had to see both of them. The first one featured the young nymphette mermaids (ages eighteen to twenty-two), and they are truly delightful looking. Sitting in the dark underwater theater, I reverted to being five years old, completely under the spell of the watery story, the music, and the fabulous fishy choreography. The girls swirl and splash, their long hair flows around their faces, and they breathe from a tube that looks like a garden hose. (Please do not attempt this at home.) At the end of each scene, a curtain of bubbles covers the glass partition, and seconds later, the mermaids reappear in their sparkling new outfits. This makes a great case for water aerobics. Their abs are as flat as ironing boards. Their backs ripple with muscle. Plus, those shimmery tails are the ultimate bling accessory.

The second show featured the "former" mermaids, from the '50s, '60s, and '70s. Now, I don't mean to be unkind, but my first thought was manatees in motion. Nevertheless, they were surprisingly graceful, and being here feels like the world has rolled slowly backwards in time. And after witnessing the most recent horrors in the news, it's a welcome relief to see that people around here have a positive antidote with a flick of their tails. After the shows, we went tubing in the chilly springs. Seventy-two degrees is very cool, but at least no one laughed at me in my bathing suit.

Life is good! Love to you all.

Alexa
Aka Trailer Trash

Oh, yes. A business sign seen on Route 441 (the scenic but slow route).
"Lava Lava Land. Our love flows for Jesus."
So, I'm goin' with the flow. Ocala is next.

The Burning Bush
Saturday, June 26, 2004

Maybe Moses really was a prophet. After all, he saw the bushes burning thousands of years ago, but he just didn't have a camera like Michael Moore to capture it. What am I talking about? Michael Moore, the recent Cannes Film Festival winner who was once described as "the kind of guy who could talk Hitler into hosting a bar mitzvah." And *Fahrenheit 9/11*, his scathing documentary film about George Bush and his cronies.

We've all seen movies that are memorable, life-changing, or just fun favorites. I've always thought that part of the impact—or lack of—was where and with whom we shared the experience. And then the big daddy of movies, possibly the most controversial movie of the decade, shown currently in only 500 theaters around the country, shows up in the 100-seat fine arts theater in Asheville, NC. Why is this such a unique happening? Well, geographically, Asheville sits at the feet of the Blue Ridge Mountains, 865 miles from Miami Beach. Socially and culturally, it's got the Bible Belt on one side and the granola gang on the other. Alternative lifestyles live here, as do born-agains and teetotalers. The people-watching includes tattooed, tie-dyed, Birkenstock-wearing, pierced, zoned-out radicals wearing no underwear, American gothic couples in denim overalls, and the organic Earth Day celebraters. "Melting pot" doesn't begin to describe the crowd, even if pot does.

So, the movie opened yesterday, and we decided we had the best chance of seeing it without crowds if we went to the 4:30 show. It was raining. It was a workday. It was Asheville, for God's sake. Quiet, little alternative Asheville. Holy Moses (pun intended), the line was already halfway back to the next town, and it was two and a half hours before the show began. We stood in the line. We spoke to more strangers in two hours than we do in Miami in two years.

Who was in the line? A minister and his wife, who proudly told me she had organized two groups of red hat ladies in Chapel Hill, two musicians from Manhattan who were performing that night with the Brevard symphony but had to see the film, a lesbian with a purple mohawk, teenagers, seniors, golfers, farmers, artists, and Trailer Trash. Craig was giving out water and organizing the lineup. I was interviewing the crowd. If you still don't know what I'm talking about, then you really must come out from under your rock and go see the movie. Rex Reed loved it. Ebert gave it several thumbs-ups. And I only wish the people who need to see it would. But you all, please go, get the messages, and pass them on. This movie pushes more buttons than the elevator in the Empire State Building. 'Nuff said. Hope to hear from you after you see it.

Love to you all.

Alexa
Aka Trailer Trash

Local Lingo in North Carolina

Going postal:

This means driving to the post office without air-conditioning, finding a parking space immediately, being the only person in line, seeing a blonde, blue-eyed postmistress who knows your name and apologizes for her bad mood.

Going shopping:

The store is open, but there are no salespeople. They are next door chatting about the weather and drinking a freshly brewed glass of sweet tea. You select the item you want, fill out the receipt yourself, with tax included, and leave a note that says "I just couldn't wait anymore."

Tent sale: The local women are selling their dresses

Favorite names of roads around town:

>Lickskillet
>Bearwallow
>Upper and Lower Pig Pen
>Possum Trot
>Bandana
>Hardscrabble
>Sleepy Hollow (our road)

Love to you all.

Alexa
Aka Trailer Trash

Estonian Husband Won't Tell Wife to Get Off His Back
July 8, 2004

Okay, it's the North Carolina wife-carrying competition! This tops chili cook-offs, marathon pole sitting, hog-calling, coleslaw wrestling (although this is a close second), and swamp buggy racing. Never before have women looked so unattractive. Never before have men regretted matrimony more.

As an extended part of the July 4th celebration in Burnsville, North Carolina, a 250-yard obstacle course is set up in the charming town square. Couples are lured into the competition by being promised local fame and their wife's weight in watermelon. Hope they all have pickup trucks. That being said, fourteen couples entered and paid a $25.00 fee.

Here's what happens:

The sole equipment that may be used by the husband is a belt so the "rider" has something to hold onto. The wives, wearing helmets, fling themselves over the husband's shoulders, butts-up (some the size of Montana), and they squeeze their thighs around the man's face while hanging down his back and holding on to the belt. This puts them about eye level with "the crack," and this position is called "the Estonian carry." Other carries include the piggyback and the firemen's carry. During this timed event, the wives resemble possums popping out of their pouches as the husbands navigate the course like frightened deer straining under the weight of too many biscuits and gravy. The ultimate humiliation occurs when the wife pretends to be whipping the husband to go faster and yells, "Giddy up!"

It occurs to me that most of these husbands have not carried their wives since the "across the threshold" moment. But this event requires a different kind of threshold—one for pain and humiliation, and of course, watermelon pits.

With the EMS and divorce lawyers standing by, the festivities continued until one couple faltered and the woman fractured her elbow. While my jaw was still hanging open in amazement, I learned that the wife-carrying competition takes its cue from an Estonian local legend about villagers who stole wives from rivals in neighboring villages. The original competitions and competitors started in Finland (no wonder they drink so much vodka there) and somehow got past airport security into the United States. Singles should not feel left out or discriminated against because competition rules state that the participating couples do not actually have to be married. But it sure helps to be close! Wish I hadn't been.

Love to you all, and thanks for writing.

Alexa
Aka Trailer Trash

July 22, 2004
Go Cat, Go

Are you someone who knows who wrote "Who Put the Bomp in the Bomp, Bomp, Bomp"? *Do you remember the name of Elvis's backup singers?* Have you ever swooned for a matinee idol, stood during an entire rock concert and screamed 'til you were hoarse, or kissed a photo of the Beatles? Well, even if you've never done or known any of these things, you will love the Rock and Roll Hall of Fame. We're in Cleveland, Ohio, and the streets are strumming with nine-foot-tall guitar statues. Each one is artistically painted, similar to the flamingos on parade in Miami a few years ago.

The Rock Hall building looks like a series of glass pyramids and sits overlooking Lake Erie, near the Cleveland Browns stadium. Once inside, sights and senses are bombarded with memorabilia of every person, place, or thing that contributed to what we now know as rock and roll. From Bob Dylan to Bob Marley, from Mahalia Jackson to the Jackson 5, from Les Paul to Paul Simon, the museum represents and tells the story of every era and the ongoing evolution of R&R. We covered six floors in five hours. In addition to the permanent collection of films, photos, and interactive jukeboxes, there was also an Annie Leibovitz photo exhibit and an entire floor dedicated to The Supremes' sparkly stage dresses. Throughout all of this, T-Rex was showing off his immeasurable dancing and singing skills, which is probably the main reason dinosaurs became extinct.

As a former regular teen dancer on Bill Wyler's Ten's Bandstand in Miami, I always knew that rock and roll was here to stay, but it's nice to know that the corporate sponsors of the world thought it worthy enough to build this place in 1983. For me, music has always represented a timeline of life events. If you've ever had the experience of hearing the first few notes of a certain song that instantly transports you to another place and time or gotten the chills when your favorite band walks onstage, you've felt the true essence of rock and roll. Good for you!

Now, I've got to get out in that trailer and bake, sauté, and broil.

Love to you all.

Alexa
Aka Trailer Trash

*Barry Mann
**The Jordanaires

July 20, 2004
The Roads Most Traveled

Many of us remember childhood road trips and seeing the world away from home from the back bench seat (I'm dating myself) of the family car, station wagon, whatever. Memories aside, I really never thought I would be rediscovering America again in an aluminum sardine can.

And so somewhere between sixty-seven thousand acres of four-foot-high corn, and fields of periwinkle-blue bachelor button flowers, I find myself in the town of Jackson Center, Ohio, one hour north of Dayton. We're here on purpose to tour the original, one and only Airstream factory, to count churches, tractors, and American flags. I've run out of fingers for all. The town of 1,300 people is immaculate in a movie set kind of way. There's not a high-rise in sight, and the only traffic light is at the main intersection between the single picture show for $2.50 and Phil's Market. Every perfectly painted house has a front porch, but since there's not much to see, I guess at the end of the day, folks catch fireflies and look at the stars.

If you've ever sat at the edge of a cornfield, a beach, or overlooking the mountains, where there were no city lights to detract from the starlight, you know how it dazzles. Here, the galaxies are no longer just a concept but more like a white river overhead. They appear so close, I swear I could put my toe in. The stars shine down on the rows of silver Airstreams that are lined up like chorus girls in silver sequins just outside the factory. If ever an alien nation has been established somewhere, it looks like this. The two-hour factory tour reinforced my admiration for Airstream, which, according to our guide, is quickly becoming a favorite of the younger generation, Hollywood celebs, and TV commercials. This American icon is made one at a time, hands on, by four hundred employees who live in this town. Alcoa supplies the aluminum; the people supply the craftsmanship.

The factory has almost 500 units backordered but refuses to add a second shift. The same crew works on one trailer through to completion, and they don't want any second-shift people coming in and causing confusion. Fortunately, greed and mass production have not arrived in Jackson Center . . . yet.

Back to the landscape for just a moment. As I look out on the perfectly symmetrical fields of crops, it occurs to me that the stripes in the American flag should represent the farmlands and the thousands of straight rows of corn, wheat, and beans. And the stars? Well, maybe they're just fireflies.

Love to you all.

Alexa
Aka Trailer Trash

P.S. "It Ain't Home 'Till You Take the Wheels Off." (Song by Antsy McClain.)

Kentucky Woman
July 25, 2004

We've heard of instant coffee, instant access, and instant gratification, but what about instant friendship? Last year in a shoe store, I unexpectedly bonded with a total stranger from Kentucky. While trying on strappy hot-pink sandals, we quickly exchanged some personal histories, and right then and there I felt that I had found a new friend. What attracts people to one another, I can't say for sure, but for me, woman's intuition plays a huge part, and I always trust mine. Plus, my new friend had three attributes that got my attention: huge blue-green eyes, a sensational smile, and a molasses-tempo Southern accent. We made our purchases, took each other's phone numbers, and said our goodbyes.

"Call me if you ever come to Louisville," she said.

"Call me next year when you come to Miami."

And then we walked in opposite directions, back to our lives.

End of story . . . until yesterday when T-Rex and I left Ohio and crossed over the Kentucky state line. "Should I call? Would she remember me? I asked T-Rex for his opinion. Big mistake.

"You mean, you met a woman at a shoe store once, and now you're going to call her? It must be a Jewish thing."

What can I say? It's not like traveling with Ann Landers. But in spite of him, I called her.

One ring . . . What if she's out of town? Two rings . . . Maybe her husband will answer, and he won't have a clue who I am. Three rings . . . The molasses voice answered. I told her who I was, and I could visualize the blue-green eyes flashing recognition. I could hear the smile in her voice as she realized who was calling. High-five for intuition!

And then the fun really began. She had a million questions. "Where are you? How soon will you be here? Do you want to stay with us? Can we have lunch and dinner? Do you think your Airstream trailer can go down the road to our horse farm?"

Let me introduce you to Elaine and Bert, the epitome of Southern hospitality. She grew up on a farm and won several championships (with the photos and ribbons to prove it) for showing her horses. He's a retired banker. They've been married fifty-one years and are now into racing and breeding as a business. They've had some wonderful stakes winners and have had horses at Gulfstream Racetrack, which is why I met her in Miami in the first place. They live in Buckner, right next to the historic town of LaGrange. Louisville is about twenty-five minutes away.

We went to their farm, which is a picturesque sixty-six acres, complete with llamas, Sicilian donkeys, a miniature horse, an authentic log home from the 1800s, a heated pool, two dogs, two cats, one golf cart, and Sydney, the talking bird who kept singing the first line of "God Bless America." After dinner in

LaGrange, where the train still runs right through the middle of Main Street, we all had Dairy Queen and took our new friends over to the Airstream, which was parked in the Walmart parking lot. FYI, we stayed in a motel, not at Walmart, because the nights are warm and our AC needs a generator to work if we aren't connected in an RV park.

They took us on a tour of the beautiful and large horse farms in the area, including the Hermitage, where Queen Elizabeth stayed. But the best was seeing their newest filly, a two-month-old potential champion, who trotted right up to us. Her little nose felt like velvet, and we all enjoyed the petting and nuzzling.

It was finally the end of a wonderful day. We exchanged mobile numbers and addresses, and this time, I know we'll see each other again. Craig has already promised Bert a flying adventure back in Miami, and Elaine and I will have a fabulous lunch and go shopping. Back on the road, I can visualize the reflection of the Kentucky bluegrass in Elaine's eyes and her smile—a smile that comes from living a satisfied life in a beautiful place, doing the things she loves with the people she loves. I'm sure she has attracted many friends over the years, and I'm just lucky to have been shoe shopping when I was. Kentucky woman meets Trailer Trash, and this time, if the shoe fits, a new friendship is formed.

Thank you, Elaine and Bert.

Love to you all.

Alexa
Aka Trailer Trash

July 28, 2004
MapQuest

What's it like on the road, sitting in the big diesel truck, anywhere from two to five hours on our travel days? Most of our time is spent listening to XM Satellite radio or CDs, stopping for stretching and bathroom breaks, snacking, and seeing anything of interest that we want to explore. Our conversation is usually idle chitchat, funny and friendly, except for one subject when I can feel the frost form on my persona as soon as it's mentioned. And that is . . . directions!

As soon as T-Rex asks something like, "How many miles is it from St. Louis to Lincoln, Nebraska?" the big chill begins to form on my brain and my heart. I'm not a great map reader, and sometimes those pages look just like bloodshot eyes with all those red lines running every which way, but I am getting better, and once in a while, I even get it right.

In order to answer the mileage question, I begin my MapQuest ritual. Not since the Invasion of Normandy has this much preparation taken place. First, I have to find the Walmart Road Atlas, which is usually buried under five motorcycle jackets in the back seat. Next, I have to find my reading glasses and a clean tissue to wipe off the traces of bean dip. Then I have to find Missouri. I'm hoping that sometime during this preliminary search T-Rex will summon his inherent GPS and figure it out without even looking at a map, which he does all the time. But no such luck this time. Fortunately, I was able to call on all my map reading skills and charted our miles, as well as our route from Iowa into Nebraska. I even highlighted the highways with my bright yellow magic marker.

By my thumb-digit calculations, we would be in Lincoln, Nebraska, by nighttime. I would advise T-Rex as we traveled. So pleased was I with this accomplishment that I allowed the small bumps in the road to lull me into a catnap—something I rarely do. And now I say, "If you slumber, you blunder."

When I woke up, T-Rex was heading due north instead of west, and we were still in Iowa and about 75 miles off course. I had slept through the advisory. He wasn't angry at all (although, I was) because now he had the opportunity to give me the lecture about how women know nothing about navigation and how it's a good thing I wasn't on the Lewis and Clark Expedition because they never would've gotten to the Pacific Ocean.

I hoped for the lecture to end and for the "Welcome to Nebraska" sign to appear. That wasn't to happen until the next day. But that night, I was vindicated. When we pulled into our space in the RV park in Council Bluffs, Iowa, Craig realized that he had left our $225.00 power cord on the ground in St. Charles, MO. Under normal circumstances, I might've been a little miffed because not having that electrical umbilical cord means no air-conditioning, tv, or microwave. Just the overhead lights. But I was overjoyed. This error was the ultimate antifreeze, and finally, T-Rex had goofed, too. I guess he is human, after all.

I withheld the lecture about how men never pay attention to anything and usually rush off without double-checking their surroundings. But I did laugh myself to sleep and dreamt of freeways and road maps all designed by women with fashion accessories dotting all the important interstates and waypoints.

Love to you all.

Alexa
Aka Christy Columbus

P.S. I always write things down so I can remember them. Now, if only I could remember where I put my pen.

Shaggy Dog Story — Maybe...
July 29, 2004

The *New York Herald* ran an article on April 21, 1912, that tells the story of a Newfoundland dog, much like the one on the Lewis and Clark Expedition, that saved many lives after the sinking of the *Titanic*. The story tells about the dog owned by Lieutenant William Murdock, the first officer of the cruise ship, *Titanic*. The dog's name was Rigel, and he was big and black. When the *Titanic* sank, Rigel kept swimming in circles looking for his drowned master. When the rescue ship, the *Carpathia*, came on the scene, it would've rammed one of the lifeboats if it weren't for Rigel's barking. Although many lives were lost to the frigid sea, Rigel was in fine shape after swimming in the cold water for hours. This same breed is also noted in another historical moment.

In 1814, Napoleon was in exile on the island of Elba. One night, Napoleon and his men carried out a plan to escape. Part of this plan was to hop on a ship and head to the mainland of France. During the fighting, Napoleon slipped off the ship and fell into the sea. His accident went unnoticed because of the noise and scuffles. It was a Newfoundland dog that went to his rescue and pulled him up and out of the water. His life was saved, and he went on to meet his Waterloo (pun intended).

One of our employees at Target Trailer used to bring his Newf to work every day. It was the largest dog I had ever seen other than a Great Dane and completely out of his element in hot Miami. He spent all day spread-eagle on the tile floor in the office, which probably still wasn't cool enough to keep him comfortable. He only barked one time that I remember, and that shook the entire parts showroom. They're calm but mighty animals, and it's fun to read about them now as important historical lifeguards.

If you're a boater, and after reading this are tempted to purchase one, Meriwether Lewis purchased his Newfoundland, "Seaman," for $20.00. Today's price is close to $1,500.00.

Additional trivia:

Meriwether Lewis committed suicide at age thirty-five. Charles Clark was a redhead. The fences of Kentucky horse farms are painted brown these days because it's cheaper and easier to maintain. Calumet Farms in Lexington is the only one with white fences. Winston Churchill gave his "Iron Curtain" speech in Missouri. Augie Busch (Mr. Budweiser) bought Daniel Boone's family farm and has turned it into an animal sanctuary. (I'll drink to that.) St. Louis is the home of the first ice cream cone.

More from the road. Love to you all.

Alexa
Aka Trailer Trash

The Mormon Conquest
July 30, 2004

Salt Lake City, Utah, has a Stepford Wife quality about it. It's a perfectly designed city on a north, south, east, west grid that is so easy to understand, even I can't get lost. All the streets are extra wide boulevards, and there's a trolley that runs through downtown to make getting from point A to B easy. It's immaculately clean and orderly, at least on the surface. However, judging from the latest news, underneath the surface has the same problems as any other city. But it is a beautiful place with flowers blooming everywhere and polite smiles on every face.

Since we arrived, we've explored Park City and Deer Valley Ski Resort, and Sundance Resort, where I was desperately seeking Robert Redford and several local boutiques and "pubs." Actually, I don't think drinking is on any Mormon's list of things to do, but I sampled a dark and malty brown beer called Polygamy Porter, and it is delicious. After I finished it, some of the men started to *look* a little like Redford.

Regardless of my religious beliefs, I respect the Mormons for what they have accomplished. As the first pioneers, they schlepped across the mountains from the east, established an entire city, and have attracted thousands of followers who have felt "the calling" from all over the world. Plus, after seeing Temple Square and the buildings it contains, they appear to be one of, if not the richest, religious groups on the planet.

The square is more like a religious fortress built from granite and marble. The church doesn't allow visitors unless they have a referral from the bishop. All very clandestine. The church towers over the square and is completely walled in. A free tour was given to us by a lovely, soft-spoken girl from Lithuania. Our guide gave us a crash course in Mormon and the Latter-Day Saints, known as LDS. From the look in the eyes of some of the "sisters," maybe it's really LSD.

Anyway, you may have noticed their newly constructed temple on Miami Beach on Indian Creek, right before 71st Street. I definitely got the feeling that anyone on the premises is fair game for conversion, but we resisted.

On Thursday evenings, the Mormon Tabernacle Choir rehearses for their internationally-heard Sunday broadcasts. The tabernacle building seats six thousand people, and we were in the sixth row. Believe it or not, it was filled to about eighty-five percent capacity. The acoustics are near perfection. The pipe organ—one of the largest in the world—has over 1,150 pipes. The pipes are gold and framed by ornate wooden carved columns. They look like tall gold whistles, but the sounds are like Enya on steroids. The choir has 320 members, all Mormons. Singers must audition and train before being accepted, and at age sixty, they are retired. Guess they haven't heard that sixty is the new forty.

The voices fill the 150-year-old building, and for a music

lover like me, they could've been singing about taking out the garbage, and I would've loved it. This was a thrill of a lifetime, and the fact that we traveled 4,600 miles to hear it made it that much more special.

I understand that all these free tours, concerts, etc., are targeted at gaining "followers," but the music is spectacular for any reason. Just in case the city, the smiles, the flowers, the tours, the music, and all the volunteer greeters and "sisters" don't convince you that the Mormon religion is a must, when you leave the tabernacle at 9:30 pm, you're greeted with an illuminated Jesus the size of Godzilla. The colorful image is standing in a stained-glass window across the courtyard, white-robed with open arms, beckoning and welcoming visitors to the fold. I immediately nicknamed him Disco Jesus.

It's all perfectly staged. You've got to give them credit for that . . . and then get the hell out of there before they take ten percent of your income.

Love to you all.

Alexa
Aka Trailer Trash

Utah — Eau de Saline
July 31, 2004

The worst thing you can do in southern Utah is walk on, hike, drive on, or otherwise break the cryptobiotic crust—a fragile and ancient covering that looks brown and crumbly and nurtures virtually all desert life. One careless step with the Nikes can destroy crust that will take fifty to one hundred years to recover. The locals say, "Tiptoe through the crypto." Good reason to stay in the air-conditioned trailer since it was 101 degrees here yesterday. But no, we had to venture on to the Great Salt Lake.

Bobbing like a cork in the lake is one of the "I did it" experiences you can talk about when you get home, so this is a sneak preview.

The lake is five times saltier than the ocean, making floating totally effortless, no matter your size. And then there is the smell. Marcel Rochas, creator of couture and fragrance, thought the "Scent of a Woman" should precede her appearance. Perhaps this is also true for lakes. We experienced the lake from Antelope Island, the largest one in the lake area. Aside from the stunning visual, the smell of brine can knock you flat.

Nothing much can live in the saline-perfumed water except the brine flies and brine shrimp that the hundreds of birds there feed on. I didn't see any shrimp, but the flies (which don't bother humans) were so dense that I thought they were patches of brown fabric on the sand and hovering over the water.

We floated for quite a while, and when we got out, we had a film of salt on us that I could have scraped off and put in a shaker. Cold showers are right next to the beach, and our skin felt really silky after we rinsed off. And did I mention the six hundred bison, mule deer, antelope, coyotes, and bighorn sheep? Yes, they roam the island, too. A dip in the Great Salt Lake is a quick way to rediscover your sense of primal joy. For an hour, or just a minute on the water, your mind and all un-civil civilization is blotted out by the silence, the bobbing, and the clean horizon, and suddenly, the smell is just part of the natural world. It sure beats the smell of exhaust and garbage trucks. Now, where is my Shalimar?

Love to you all.

Alexa
Aka Trailer Trash

Forgotten Tidbits
August 1, 2004

In Nebraska, we stayed at an unusual RV park. Right on the premises, and within walking distance from our space, was the world headquarters of a store called Cabela's. In case you've never heard of it, it's on the same order of Outdoor World off I-95 at Stirling Road. Its four-inch catalog is full of fishing tackle, camping equipment, and hunting paraphernalia. All the manly stuff. Somewhere between the life-size stuffed grizzlies and home truth video about spring turkey shooting, we entered the gun department, a sacred sanctuary where men drop to their knees at the sight of boxes of ammunition and hundreds of weapons. Now, picture five grown men lusting over a $4500.00, .50-caliber sniper rifle, gazing at it as if it were the Mona Lisa and they were in the Louvre.

And now for the classic remark of the day . . . I asked one of the men, "What do you do with that?"

His reply was, "Reach out and touch someone."

After that, I wandered off, dazed by the amount of testosterone in the store, and walked directly into the aisle of chocolate moose droppings, sold by the bag. Even though the bag said they were really malt balls, I couldn't quite bring myself to sample them. Would you?

Joke of the day, told to me by a Mormon, but not a terribly religious one.

"What's the difference between a Mormon wife and an elephant?"

Fifteen pounds.

"How do you make them equal?"

Force-feed the elephant.

The bad news! Our mail, which has been forwarded successfully to us all over the country with absolutely no problem, has either been lost or stolen. T-Rex has filed a police report, but I have a feeling it won't get much attention because of the Lori Hacking search in the Salt Lake landfill.

Putting it all in perspective, losing our mail really isn't the end of the world, but if any of you have sent me anything really important, like $$$, the map to buried treasure, an invitation to a great party, or a love letter, please resend.

Love to you all.

Alexa
Aka Trailer Trash

Drilling-Blasting-Hauling-Crushing

You may need earplugs.

The Bingham Canyon Mine, which is more than three quarters of a mile deep and 2.5 miles wide, is just one of two man-made objects on Earth that can be seen by astronauts from outer space. The other is the Great Wall of China. We visited it today and saw firsthand the world's first and largest open-pit copper mine. Just how big is big? The Sears Tower, at 1,454 feet tall, would reach only halfway up the mine. And without giving you all the statistics, the one that really describes just how much copper is produced at the Kennecott Mine was this one: it's enough to wire all the houses in Canada, Mexico, and the United States. This is a state-of-the-art facility and a company that is ecologically sensitive. It works with and protects the environment and supports hundreds of charities and the cultural arts. Sounds like marriage material to me.

By the way, practically everything we use has some copper in it—our hairdryers, computers, cookware, and automobiles, to name a few. And there's "gold in them thar hills." Bingham Canyon ore has yielded more than 17 million tons of copper, 23 million ounces of gold, and 190 million ounces of silver—

more than the total yields of the Comstock Lode, Klondike, and California Gold rushes combined. That's a lot of bracelets and earrings, but there were no free samples. So now I've started to take notice of copper, and out West, I've seen the burnished flash of copper roofs. When the sun hits them, it looks like someone just lit a large match. Really pretty!

Before leaving what is called "The Richest Hole on Earth," we stood at the mine overlook about 6,700 feet above sea level, and I could see, hear, and feel the magnitude of the excavations. Originally a mountain, the mine looks like a huge bowl carved out in concentric circles in slate blue, pale rust, and taupe. From this view, the huge trucks used for hauling look like Tonka toys traversing the carved rims. In fact, they are gigantic pieces of equipment with 20-foot-high tires that each cost $20,000. I can't imagine how they change one of them, but I bet they don't call AAA.

Okay. Mr. Wizard is signing off for a while. I need to recover my hearing.

Love to you all.

Alexa
Aka Trailer Trash

One Step up from the Manger
August 4, 2004

On a cool starry night, two weary travelers in a truck, pulling an Airstream trailer, arrived late in West Yellowstone, Montana, and there were no rooms at the inns—Holiday, Comfort, Best Western, Hibernation Station, Stagecoach, and so on. There were also no places at the local RV parks, Grizzly and Roundup. And for the first time, when a Walmart parking lot might've been an overnight option, there was no Walmart. There was, however, Sagebrush Floral and The Trout Shop on what promised to be a very unusual main street.

What was a Jewish princess to do? Well, this one closed her eyes and envisioned the Fontainebleau Hotel, and lo and behold, a vision appeared. It was the three wise men of the West: two Harley riders and a fly fisherman. They pointed east to a brightly lit neon sign in the sky that was only missing five letters. Having been a *Wheel of Fortune* watcher, I was able to guess correctly at the phrase: "motel vacancy."

T-Rex grabbed the very last room, sight unseen. He unlocked the door. I was afraid to look. I looked. Apparently, I had guessed incorrectly. The correct phrase was "the Manger."

And if there is a babe to be born here, he'd better like a stale-smelling room with bullet holes in the wall.

We are now in Spearfish, South Dakota, fifteen minutes away from Sturgis, the scene of the 64th annual motorcycle rally. They're expecting 500,000 bikers. I wrote about this last year, so I won't repeat except to say that if any of you single girlfriends want to find a guy, this is the place. The ratio is about twenty to one. And in spite of their outwardly grunge look, many of them are successful businessmen, well educated, and personable. Oh, yeah. And a lot of them are just plain disgusting, too.

This area has lots going for it. There is a ton of history of the Old West. The Black Hills are magnificent without being as scary as the Rockies. Deadwood is fifteen minutes away if you like gambling, and Kevin Costner can be found many nights there at his club or at Titonka, his ode to the bison museum. Plus, there are gold mines, Mount Rushmore, and Devils Tower.

I'll see you all soon, but 'til then, picture miles and miles of open forest surrounded by the outline of the Black Hill peaks, and then repeat the mantra of the motorcycle riders all over the world: "Giddy up, steel horse. A flick of the wrist on the throttle makes the white lines disappear and your spirit fly. It's not just a road you're riding on, it's a path to freedom."

Love to you all.

Alexa
Aka Trailer Trash

2005

She's Gone Again!
June 11, 2005

Headline: Jewish Princess Becomes Trailer Trash for the Fourth Time!

Please don't take this personally, but I can't wait to get outta here. Why? Well, unless your Ray-Bans have fogged over from the humidity, you've probably noticed the changing skyline of Miami—more construction cranes than clouds, and water views are harder to find than a winning basketball team (oh, that was so cruel).

And then there's the traffic. Along with a hard hat, a cell phone, and mascara, I drive with a death grip on the wheel. Each day, I've used all my Grand Prix skills to navigate through the newly created gridlock. As I look around through the detours, there appears to be something happening that is even more frightening than George Bush for another four years. It's an encroaching sameness of stores, condos, and fast-food places. It's as if peer pressure now exists in the world of shopping, dwellings, and eating. The fact is, I almost fainted a few years ago when I saw the golden arches on the Champs d'Elysée . . . mon Dieu! It's here, it's there, it's global. And so, before another sleek highrise or Banana Republic store pops up like a groundhog on yet another trendy street, I must pack my rhinestone tiara and venture out. We will take a break from America the monoculture and head for greener pastures.

In my trashy opinion, individuality is now heading for the newly endangered species list. So, before it completely disappears, I hope to rediscover America the unique, the overlooked—and please, God of adventure—the underdeveloped. While I'm away, I'm going to eavesdrop on small-town conversations. I'm going to relish every one-story building I see. I'm going to overindulge in homemade cooking, when I can find it. I'm going to enjoy every unpaved rut in the back roads, and I'm going to soak up the spirit of American individuality while it's still there. And I know it is!

Please don't misunderstand. I love Miami, all of you, and all the cool things we have here, but it's around this time of year that all the potholes in our city and our society accumulate in my psyche, and just like an automobile, I need a mind/body alignment—the serenity of a clear mountain lake, a country store instead of the Gap, a bowl of blueberry buckle instead of tiramisu, and some conversations with strangers. If you like, I'll share it all with you. Please keep in touch, because you know I miss you all. I'll have my cell phone, my laptop, and my muse—the indomitable T-Rex.

My love to you all. Have a terrific summer, and take pictures of Biscayne Bay. You may want to look at it sometime in the future.

Love to you all.

Alexa
Soon to be "Trailer Trash"

"Rainy Night in Georgia"
June 18, 2005

Well, this is different. T-Rex is driving the truck with the trailer, and I'm driving his new Chrysler 300, aka "the Hemi." We'll leave the car in Burnsville when we hit the road, but in the meantime, I was at the wheel of this velvet beast for 875 miles. Just turning on the radio requires two weeks of ground school. Air-conditioning is another learned skill, and the navigation system is as complicated as the cockpit of a jet.

So, here I am at highway speeds, one hand and eye on the road, the other fumbling around with all the buttons, just to get cool air. We stop at the first rest stop, and I explain this to T-Rex,

He is astonished. "Didn't you read the manual? It's the first thing I do."

Excuse me. The manual is ninety-seven pages long. It's in English, but it might as well be a foreign language. And besides, I'd rather read *Vanity Fair*.

T-Rex is horrified that I have not yet mastered the cruise control or delighted in the joys of the cursor on the bright, intrusive GPS map. He starts to explain some of the functions, and I start thinking that this could be one of our shorter trips together, but I make a quick exit to the bathroom. When I come out, he's surrounded by a group of men, all of them with that special glazed look they get when they see a '56 Chevy, or any vehicle with an abundance of chrome. And then I hear it.

"Is that a hemi?"

Just like the ad on TV. Yep. I wanted America, and I've already found it. So far, it's overweight and wearing black socks with shorts, but it's enthusiastic about cars and speaks English . . . sort of.

After an eight-hour drive, we decided to stay in a motel instead of an RV park in Tifton, GA. With all the hip clubs and celebrities we see in Miami, it was nice to know that Tifton has some, too. Just our luck, staying right on our floor was the Miss Forestry Queen of Atkinson County. How did I know that? Well, she had a huge poster Scotch Taped to the front of her door, with two life-size pictures of herself—one in a purple evening gown, and one with her bowling ball.

It was pouring down rain, but we decided to gas up so we'd be ready to roll early. Apparently, the gas station is one of the hot spots in town, so we had to wait our turn at the pumps. Just as we were about to start filling up, a Southern voice came out over the loudspeaker, kind of like the principal when we were in elementary school, minus the accent.

"Hold yer pumping. We're fixin' to drop the price three cents."

Well, the woman at the next pump gave out a "Praise the Lord!" that would've made Fran Drescher sound like the Horse Whisperer. We found out there was a price war going on and filled up for $1.95 a gallon (that's regular). My "Praise the Lord" was just a little softer.

On the way to Atlanta (Scarlett and my nieces were waiting), I noticed that there wasn't any retail therapy to be had on I-75. It's all discount outlet malls. They sell everything from hardwood floors to Bibles. But somewhere in between the Lee jeans and the Claxton fruitcakes, I saw the best billboard ever: a huge, green, grinning Shrek that reads "Ogre achiever! Believe in yourself! Pass it on!"

I'll second that.

Love to you all.

Alexa
Aka Trailer Trash

Beauty and the Born-Agains
June 16, 2005

Greetings from the starch capital of the world, where Bojangles says their chicken is "born and breaded," where Hardees says "think thick," and KFC calls themselves the "original thigh master." (Sorry, Suzanne Sommers.) But enough about health food.

Not an intolerant person, I've always respected the beliefs of others, and in some ways admired those who have a strong faith that helps them in difficult times.

Here in Burnsville, North Carolina, there are more churches and beauty salons than there are Italian restaurants on South Beach. It's a little town where the beauty industry is as large as the women and where "You know you're trailer trash if your wife's hairdo was once ruined by a ceiling fan." It's a dry county with a lot of alcoholics and a local newspaper that has a daily column written by Billy Graham, who is constantly mentioning Satan and salvation. It seems that the churches are the country clubs of small towns, the social center of all life's passages from birth to death, but still, I was a little taken aback when I went to buy an iron in town and found that the Bible Belt had expanded to other articles of clothing.

As I entered the not-so-special "specialty" store called Roses, that sells everything from camping equipment to knee-highs, I stopped in my tracks, right in front of a rack of T-shirts that said: "Coffee gets me started. Jesus keeps me going." These shirts are manufactured by a company called Higher Level Apparel. So, with an even higher awareness and a new iron, I started noticing the special signs of the times around here: "Be an organ donor. Give your heart to God." "Don't just commit. Submit to the Lord." "Hell is an awful place, but we don't have to go there." "Trouble? Read the directions." (This one had a picture of the Holy Bible.) "Our church is prayer-conditioned." And my personal favorite: "Firefighters rescue. Only Jesus saves."

But then I found out that this religious experience is enjoying an off-Broadway run in New York in a show called *Altar Boyz*. It's an energetic musical about a Christian boy band out to save the souls of its audience. Its "Raise and Praise" tour is currently in NYC.

I'm hoping for some equal representation for us bagel lovers. So far, the closest I've come is seeing a license plate with the sign of the fish, and across the top, the word *gefilte*. In the meantime, I'm finding my religion at a very easy yoga/tai chi class, and if the good Lord, or Lordess, is watching, I'm not using any hair spray, and my T-shirt says "Good girls don't make history."

Please go make a little history this summer, and if you do,

please write me about it. Oh, and if you run into any born-agains, ask them if they know Brian Weiss.

Love to you all.

Alexa
Aka Trailer Trash

"Mack the Knife" and the Outer Banks
June 22, 2005

Time doesn't always fly when you're a passenger in a diesel truck pulling a 34-foot sardine can. Why complain? It's just a quick nine-hour jaunt from Burnsville, NC, to the Outer Banks. North Carolina, like California, has mountains and beaches, and since I haven't been to the beach at home in years, it sounded like a good idea. But it was our pre-jaunt talk that started to fill me with dread. Why? I'm a good sport, but I'm not an athletic sport. And I'm not an early riser.

My princess hackles started to prickle when I heard we'd be leaving at 5:30 a.m. and driving 'til we got there, no matter what. As a totally misdirected enticement, T-Rex said that some of our weekend activities would include parasailing from behind a boat, sailing in a midget catamaran, hang-gliding, kite-boarding, and attending surf-riding school. If we had time, we would rent wave runners. Whoa, whoa, whoa!

My beach activities include reading, resting, shelling, walking, eating, and drinking an occasional mood-altering beverage. Let me explain . . . I love water. I love to look at it, drink it, bathe in it, and boat across it, but hanging above it at 1,000 feet is not going to happen. How was I going to dodge this watery bullet?

And then T-Rex asked, "Did you bring your bathing suit?"

Crossing my manicured fingers and conjuring up my most sincere water-loving face, I replied, "Oh no. I forgot to pack it."

"No problem," he said. "I'll buy you one."

Now we're really entering unchartered waters of a different nature. The only thing more frightening than going hang-gliding in shark-infested waters is buying a swimsuit. When was the last time any of you tried on a bathing suit in front of a three-way mirror and walked away smiling? Martinis, yes. Tankinis, no way.

You may be wondering why, as a Miami Beach native and daughter of an avid sport fisherman, I don't want to go near the ocean water, in the ocean, or engage in anything that would land me in the ocean. Please read on.

If you adhere to the theory that nothing is a coincidence, you'll appreciate what happened the night before we left. We were watching the Discovery Channel, and instead of the usual beguiling histories of the origin of popcorn-making or alien life in Detroit, the evening's program was called *Shark Attack*. The narrator proceeded to name all the beach locations where there had been shark attacks.

New Smyrna Beach has had the most, Virginia Beach and the Jersey Shore, a few. And then, as the grand finale, in gory detail, we witnessed the reenactment of a fatal attack on a child from a nine-foot bull shark, right off the Cape Hatteras beach, right along the coast of the Outer Banks. And there you have it. Count me out! The only reason I watched this horror program was to reinforce the decision I had made long ago. I do not go in the ocean. This final decision was made the day T-Rex flew me along our Florida coastline from Palm Beach to Key Biscayne. We were in a two-seater airplane, flying low, about 500 feet above the ocean, and they were down there—sharks the size of Ferraris, stingrays, and more sharks, right close to the shore, clearly within striking distance of unaware swimmers and waders.

T-Rex watched me watching the program, and he knew that nothing he could say now would convince me to put so much as a pedicured toe in the Atlantic, especially since the polish was blood red.

And though that was the end of his parasailing dreams with me, I'm pretty sure I heard him humming the first lines of "Mack the Knife" as I sweetly consented to bathing suit shopping. After a nine-hour drive, the least I can do is swim in the heated, shark-free pool. Let's hope there are no land sharks in our RV park.

Love to you all.

Alexa
Aka Trailer Trash

Pitch, Yaw, and Roll
Or How 12 Seconds Changed the World

Men and some women have always wanted to fly. Way back in Greek mythology, two brothers, Icarus and Daedalus, were so obsessed with the desire to fly that they made wings out of feathers and wax. Just flying wasn't enough for one of them who wanted to fly higher and higher, and as he did, the sun melted the wax and he crashed to the ground. The original crash and burn. Centuries later, two other brothers, bicycle builders from Dayton, Ohio, had a similar obsession.

Orville and Wilbur Wright turned feathers and wax into propellers and chains as they successfully broke the bond with Earth. Their first flight lasted twelve seconds and covered a distance less than the length of a commercial airliner: 120 feet. On December 17, 1903, the brothers dressed in coats and ties flipped a coin to see who would be positioned on the flyer. Orville won, and the rest is aviation history.

The Wright Brothers National Museum is located on the Outer Banks in the town of Kill Devil Hills, between Kitty Hawk and Nags Head. The mini airstrip, the detailed sculpture of the airplane, and the sixty-foot monument honor the brothers and the hundreds of glider flights that preceded the first powered flight. Yesterday, we stood at the exact spot where the first flight took off.

It was especially poignant to watch Craig taking it all in, picturing himself at that historic moment. If you know him at all, you know he'd rather be flying than anything else. I've never looked, but I'm sure he has a secret glove compartment with feathers and wax in it. I, on the other hand, pictured myself one hundred years ago without so many of the inventions we take for granted, and then I fast-forwarded to the present. I wondered what might be happening right now, somewhere in the world, what special achievement, by some especially obsessed person, might be changing our world twelve seconds at a time.

Things I've learned so far:

1. A new word: *koru* means spiral up. It comes from an ancient New Zealand tribe. The spa on the Outer Banks expects their treatments to elevate the body and soul. I had an acupressure manicure and pedicure and agree it was aptly named.

2. If you're walking in the dark, in the middle of a pasture, use your cell phone as a flashlight. The glow of it will light the way and attract hundreds of lightning bugs for an additional glow. Plus, it's fun!

3. Every inch of a shark's tooth is equal to ten feet of the shark's body.

4. The first English colony was started off North Carolina Outer Banks, in the town of Roanoke. At that time, Roanoke was part of Virginia, named after Queen Elizabeth I, the "Virgin Queen." Who was she kidding? She had the hots for Sir Walter Raleigh.

5. Lighthouse keepers don't live at the top of the lighthouse. They live in a house nearby and operate the necessary machinery from the ground. T-Rex walked up 268 steps, the equivalent of twelve stories, to the top of Cape Hatteras Lighthouse. And I watched him.

Love to you all.

Alexa
Aka Trailer Trash

Swashbucklers and Shipwrecks
The Outer Banks

We are currently hunkered down in the midst of 25-mile-an-hour winds and battering rains. It's the worst weather we've encountered in four years of Trailer Trash travels. Camp Hatteras RV Park is in the heart of the North Carolina Outer Banks. Pimlico Sound is to the west, across the highway, and the Atlantic is to the east, 200 feet from our Airstream. A quick step over the dunes on a wooden bridge puts your foot on the same beach where pirates and Spanish marauders stood decades ago.

Before the rains came, we motorcycled up and down the narrow grey ribbon of road that stretches a long line from Nags Head to Cape Hatteras. Hundreds of gingerbread-style houses on stilts border the shoreline in weathered, drab shades of grey and olive. Occasionally a strawberry-, lemon-, or lime-sherbet-painted house cheerfully stands tall. Lighthouses, Adirondack chairs, and hammocks are as common as cappuccinos at Starbucks.

When we first arrived, the sun was blazing bright on a comfortable 70-degree day, but our east neighbor, the moody and restless Atlantic, has turned wet and wild during the night. The rain on the Airstream's metal roof sounds like Steppenwolf in quadraphonic sound. The wind was rocking the trailer until T-Rex donned his bright yellow slicker, and like Captain Ahab, went outside to lower the awnings and secure the rear jacks. Couched safely inside, I can only imagine the sea captains years ago, their lost horizons and shipwrecks in the place where hurricanes and hardships have earned these waters the nickname, "Graveyard of the Atlantic."

The Cape Hatteras Lighthouse, with its deliberately recognizable red and white stripes, was not enough to guide pirate ships, Civil War ships, and WWII ships to safe harbor. More than six hundred ships have been lost off these shores.

Back on dry land, the north end of the banks is very commercial: Kmarts and fast foods and lots of traffic on two-way Highway 64. But the south end, with Hatteras and Ocracoke Island, provides the remote, unspoiled villages far from the rush and rest of the world. Of course, I like that part best.

As we ferried across to Ocracoke Island with the motorcycle, all I could see was water, boats, and floating islands. High-rises are taboo, and even on the developed end, the height restriction is four stories. Just before sunset, the light and the sky take on an eerie, luminous glow—one that my photographer and watercolor artist friends would enjoy trying to capture. I couldn't!

Ocracoke Inlet is the place where Edward Teach, aka Blackbeard the Pirate, was killed. It is also where this year's high school graduating class consisted of only seven students. Not a booming metropolis. Here, T-Rex parasailed, and I took photos from the boat. I had a split-second regret about not trying it. That vanished as Craig was reeled out and up, higher and higher, to a barely visible speck 1,200 feet above the water. It's said that Blackbeard married fourteen times, and he was probably also the inventor of dreadlocks. Just before he attacked his prey, he would braid his beard with red ribbons and tie live fuses to it. With his beard on fire, he looked like the devil and easily intimidated his victims. Is this where the phrase "He looks like the devil" comes from?

Speaking of looking like the devil, I bought a leopard print tankini for $10.99 in one of those tacky tourist beach shops. I refused to spend a penny more on anything that hideous. Mother Nature must have been peeking in my dressing room with horror. One look, and it hasn't stopped raining since.

Love to you all. Stay dry, and thanks for your messages.

Alexa
Aka Trailer Trash

October 12, 2005
Serendipity and Ethel

We came upon her quite by accident while visiting someone else in the neighborhood. She had been abandoned by those who used to love her and honor all her qualities. She was completely alone in the world. No one had visited her in five years. The grass had grown up at her doorstep, and her windows were darkened with dust. But still, she had proudly stood her ground. Her old bones were intact, and her hard exterior still glimmered ever so slightly, suggesting the beauty she'd been before. She was dirty, she was broken down, but still something shined through. And could we, once having seen her, in good conscience, allow her to remain neglected?

Ethel's condition is an homage to a culture that likes everything shiny and new. A culture that doesn't necessarily care for people and things that get old, except for the icons—the famous, the infamous. And so, we had a decision to make. What would we do for her? What *could* we do for her? Would she be able to move? Would she fall apart? Would she respond well if given all the TLC she really needed? Could we bring her back to her place in the world? Were we crazy to even consider it?

Our lives certainly weren't lacking responsibilities. What was the right thing to do? After many hours of discussion and several visits, we decided to give it a try.

Ours would be a small investment of time and money, with a potentially soul-satisfying reward.

And so, we bought a 1978, 31-foot, vintage Airstream trailer. I nicknamed her Ethel in honor of the 84-year-old woman who lives in the brick house just above the place where Ethel had been abandoned for half a decade. Ethel, the woman, is a tough mountain lady who reminds me of the old Airstream. She has traveled out and back on a long, hard road from the farm on which she was raised. She knows how to build anything, and through the years has provided safe places for soldiers and farmers, with houses and barns built with her own hands. She smiles a mostly toothless smile, talks like a trucker, and walks slightly crooked with the help of a stout walking stick. She brags that she could drive or ride anything with wheels—tanks, bulldozers, motorcycles, and every kind of earth-mover. She is old and arthritic but feisty. She has managed very well on her own, and unlike the Airstream, has many visitors and still keeps busy "when the arthritis isn't too bad." She said, "I don't read or write well, but I can sign my name, and I do the numbers in my head."

Ethel has good bones and a hard shell. She took a liking to us, poked us with her walking stick, and teased us about being up to the job of restoring our newly acquired vintage icon.

The whole incident was a meeting of chance . . . a serendipitous encounter. But to me, both Ethels represent a certain kind of beauty of age and a life well lived and well-constructed. I think that faded beauty deserves to be admired and cared for.

The restoration began immediately after we successfully hooked up the 31-foot trailer to Craig's truck. She towed right along to my property, where we cleaned and scrubbed her for hours. In just two days, she started to shine a little, and in three days, the musty smell was gone. In four days, the bathroom and kitchen areas were usable, and on the fifth day, we hooked up the power. To our amazement, after not being used for years, every light came on, plus the blasting eight-track, built-in stereo. John Denver was singing "Country Road" right on cue. Soul-satisfying doesn't begin to describe the feeling of accomplishment for all our hard work and for having made a good decision. And now Ethel is getting a reputation around here.

Burnsville, North Carolina, is a small town, and local people have started inquiring about her. "Is she for sale?" Not so fast! I have some special interiors planned, and she still needs new windows, flooring, and upholstery. Ethel will make a trip to Tampa for the final mechanical touches, and hopefully will arrive back in Miami in the near future. I hope you will all come by to see her. I have the before pictures, and believe me, she looked worse than many of the homes ravaged by Hurricane Katrina.

And since I mentioned vintage . . . why the attraction? Could it be that we associate these older things—music, movies, cars, clothing, grandparents—with a better, happier time? A time we want desperately to recapture so that we can feel that special era again? I don't know. But I do know that

Ethel makes me feel good right now. And even though I've ruined two manicures, it was well worth it.

Love to you all.

Alexa
Aka Trailer Trash

Memory Lane. Or, What Lasts Forever?

My longtime friend Allen has just left Burnsville after an all-too-brief visit with us. He was a perfect houseguest! He loved being here and now wants to find a place of his own—maybe a log cabin or some charming rustic retreat. So, off we went to look at a house that was listed nearby and seemed to fit his desires. The home was not quite right, but the drive took us down a beautiful country road that turned out to be memory lane for someone else. And so, I ask you . . . What do you think lasts forever?

The road is called Upper Pig Pen. We were driving along, when suddenly, an old Victorian dollhouse came into view, just like the pop-up storybooks we read to children. It looked like a tiny fairytale with flower beds of azaleas and daylilies, a wooden front porch swing, a corn crib, a pump house, and a winding little stone path to the back near the stream. The lawn was slightly overgrown, the white lace curtains were fluttering in the afternoon breeze, and there was a for-sale sign in front. That was all I needed to get me out of the truck. There didn't seem to be anyone around, so we stopped the truck and started to walk up to peek inside. Just then, a petite fairy godmother of a woman appeared. She had grey, wavy hair that framed her Doris Day face and pussy cat blue eyes. She was elderly but hardy looking.

For some reason, despite the for-sale sign, I felt like a trespasser. She seemed wary of us, two strangers walking on her property. Nervously, I started to blather on about how picturesque the house was and hoped she didn't mind that we stopped. But we had interrupted her. She was about to get the mower out and cut the overgrown grass. I introduced myself and asked her why she was selling.

She replied that her name was Lily, and she said, "Well, I don't think a woman of my age should live out here all alone."

I agreed but said nothing. After all, here she was, and not looking a bit worse for wear. I asked her the unthinkable: "How old are you?" "I'm eighty." All right. So, I don't see a lot of eighty-year-old women mowing, but I knew there was more to the story. And then she said, "It was different when my husband was here. I don't like to think about how long he's been gone." As she spoke, she twirled her narrow gold wedding band around and around her finger. Then she said, "My daughters don't think I should be here anymore. I fell a few months ago. I didn't break anything, but now they worry about me all the time, so I'm going to live near them in Tampa."

I really wanted to go inside the house, but it didn't feel like this little fairy godmother was going to share her memories with strangers. I didn't push, but I thanked her for her time and asked her if she was the original owner.

She said, "Well, almost. And if you don't mind the untidiness, you can come inside."

It was all I could do to keep from leaping in front of her. We went around to the back porch and in through the back door.

She told us how she and her husband had liked to sit back there, away from the road where nobody could see them. "We've always had does and wild cats come up to the porch. I never made a big effort to pet them, but I feed them."

The inside of the house could've been an antique store or a granny's attic. The worn furniture was covered in old rose fabric, and cross-stitch designs were everywhere. The fireplace was carved with the date 1896. And then I saw the photo on the wall—a handsome young officer in his uniform.

She saw me stare. "We married during World War Two." She looked up at me, blue eyes now misty wishing wells. "You never get over it, you know."

I said, "Yes, I know." But I kept my own story to myself.

Trying to lighten up the moment a bit, we told her we had an Airstream trailer.

They had one, too, years ago, and went on lots of group caravans, all the way to Colorado. She said, "Those were the wild days."

I saw her flashing back, and we invited her to come see ours sometime. "How about if we pick you up one afternoon? We can have dinner together, and you can see what a new one looks like?" I could tell she was flashing back again.

Her Doris Day smile narrowed, and she said politely and firmly said, "No, thank you."

We were stunned. Why would she refuse such a genuine offer? We were silent, and then she spoke.

"Some memories are too painful to . . ." And before she

could finish the sentence, I put my arm around a total stranger and was hugging her. I finished her sentence in my mind. I flashed back to those memories that I purposely don't think about. The ones that are buried under layers of then and now, and the lump in my own throat told me that maybe she was right to refuse our invitation. We all make memories every day, but certain ones are kept to ourselves—the sweet and bittersweet ones that we want to remain untouched and unchanged by someone else's words, or the ones that make us feel too vulnerable when we remember them. Those are the ones that last forever, and so I have answered my own question. What about you? What has lasted forever for you? I hope if it's a memory, it's a sweet one. I hope whether it's something funny or sad, you will be able to share it.

We said goodbye, gave her our phone numbers, and asked her to call us if she changed her mind. I'll let you know if Lily calls, but I wouldn't bet money on it.

Cherish your memories.

Love to you all.

Alexa
Aka Trailer Trash

2006

June 2006
"Tin-Can Living Becomes Fashionable"

I need a vacation from "stuff"! I knew I was over the edge as I watched myself panic when my TiVo temporarily stopped working last month. The two-hour finale of *Desperate Housewives* was just a day away, and the TiVo techies were not solving my problem. Who's the desperate one now?

And that's just one little example of how our gadgets and gizmos can cause us the same amount of anxiety that not having them used to cause. The cell phone drops a call at the most crucial moment, or worse, rings at the most crucial moment. The fax doesn't go through, but you don't know it. You can't remember your password, let alone the name of the movie you just saw, and the computers are down, but only when you need some critical info. When the "stuff" malfunctions, we wonder how we ever lived without it. Well, there's one way to find out. Hitch up the silver palace, stock up the mobile mansion, and set your sights on the long white line.

The charismatic two-lane highways are waiting, and even with the Airstream in tow, I hope to avoid the soulless interstates. I'd like a little soul in my vacation, and that hopefully includes the nearly extinct soda fountains and town squares and tacky neon-signed motels. Maybe I'll come across some of those famous monuments that we read about in high school. Maybe I'll find some kitschy little souvenir stands selling the same postcards they have for years, still thriving in our modern world. Maybe I'll find some really neat "stuff."

Plus, this year, with product placement of the Airstream trailer in TV shows like *Grey's Anatomy*, (Dr. McDreamy's pad) and Paris Hilton's *The Simple Life*, submitting to a life of wanderlust has never been more fashionable. Another hip plus for Airstream's image is that Matthew McConaughey (*People Magazine*'s choice for "this year's sexiest man") has just traveled cross-country in his 28-foot Airstream. Too bad I missed him.

On the "I can't believe I just read that" sign, there is also an orthodox rabbi from Miami Beach who travels in his Airstream and counsels married couples. "Shalom from Home" is his shtick, and last but not least, the wonderful "Story Corp" mobile units that send Airstreams around the country and collect the stories of people, just like you and me, to be archived in the Smithsonian for the future. We happened to spot the Miami unit right across from the *Miami Herald* in May, and when we went inside, it was completely outfitted as a recording studio. Never knew heavy metal could be so versatile and nurturing.

So, it's a little like running away to join the circus, but in my case, I feel like I'm running away from the local circus to join the real world.

Discovery is just around the bend. Right now, it's time to turn the truck key and head on down the road. I just hope that when we get to the fork in the road, it's sterling silver.

Love to you all. Please don't forget to call and write.

Alexa
Aka Trailer Trash

July 2006
Fireflies Lighting Up the Night

Yancey County in Burnsville, NC, is a dry county. What does that mean? It means that at the end of the day, there is no typical urban happy hour, no two-for-one well drinks, no cosmos, no mojitos, and no pick-up joints. You get the picture?

But, just around dusk, with the Blue Ridge Mountains as a backdrop, I hang out on my porch and watch as the blinking fireflies turn my front yard into a singles bar!

Oh, to be a firefly, flitting about, flashing a lighted signal of love, and all without the first sip of wine.

The male fireflies are out cruising for chicks, and if a girl firefly is impressed, she will say, "Look at the blinker on that guy." Sound familiar?

When it comes to *Lampyridae, uncommonly known as fireflies, size does matter. Just like SOBE, it's the ones with the brightest flash that get the mates. Not all fireflies flash. The lightless ones use sex-attracting pheromones, kind of like Old Spice cologne with wings. On average, it takes a male seven nights of flashing to find a female that would accept him (for mating). On the other hand, when a female wants a mate, it takes her less than ten minutes. You "glow," girl! The major communication is, "Look at me. I'm hot."

All this flitting and glowing isn't really that great because fireflies only live about two weeks in their adult state.

If you don't have the memories of catching fireflies as a kid and you're looking for something to do other than golf, tennis, or bridge, here's how to catch one:

Get a clean glass jar, but do not poke holes in the lid. If you do and you bring the jar inside where the air is dry, the firefly will dry out and die by morning.

Dampen a paper towel, and put it in the bottom of the jar, along with a few blades of long green grass for the fireflies to lounge on. Use your hands or a small net. Please be gentle, and remember that they don't bite or sting. Be sure to release your firefly first thing in the morning so they can roam the night, flashing their lights, searching for a mate in a very short life span.

I always wondered what makes a firefly light up the night. Apparently, there is some kind of chemical reaction that produces a light-emitting molecule called luciferin. Luciferin can now be synthesized and is used in glow sticks. On my porch after dark, I can see hundreds of lights sparkling, and no doubt the little winged hussies are talking dirty. Express dating has come to the Blue Ridge Mountains, and I get to watch!

Love to you all. A happy and safe July 4th. Feeling the glow . . .

Alexa
Aka Trailer Trash

*Scientific facts were taken from the works of the curator of Purdue Entomological Research Collection.

T-Rex Goes to Dollywood
July 20, 2006

Whoever said that "getting there is half the fun" obviously never traveled with T-Rex. Sometimes, getting there is no fun at all.

I'd had a bit too much of porch-sitting, so we headed out from Burnsville, North Carolina, by car, over hill and dale, past streams, away from my delicate, sexy fireflies, to the neon billboards and gaudy flashing signage of Pigeon Forge, Tennessee, home of Dolly Parton's Dollywood.

In the mid-1700s, the little settlement on the great river was widely known for its iron ore forges, natural abundance, carrier pigeons, and peaceful ways. What a difference three centuries make. Since those good old days, the carrier pigeon has become extinct (there is a stuffed example in the archives of the national parks Sugarland Museum), and the grist mills and iron works have been replaced with fudge factories, outlet malls, and tourists.

In place of the early settlers, we have a new breed of Americans. I call them the Farkels. The Farkels are from all over, but mostly the South and the Midwest. They have an abundance of body fat, usually travel in packs, and have never heard of dentistry. Farkel fashion sense consists of black socks with sandals, elastic waistbands, and large, brightly colored plastic bags filled with snacks. They are usually carrying a Tastee Freez in each hand.

Pigeon Forge is one long highway crammed full of Farkels, motels, all-you-can-eat buffets, gift shops, and musical shows. The pigeon "strip" is a Las Vegas wannabee except for the gigantic illuminated white cross that overlooks the city, rivaling the Bellagio's dancing fountains.

But we almost never got to enjoy this tacky little town because of T-Rex's superb taste in lodgings. As we drove down the strip, he asked, "Where would you like to stay?" (We had left the Airstream in Burnsville.) I replied, "The Hampton Inn." He asked, "What about this place right on the river?" I said, "I'd rather stay at the Hampton Inn." He said, "Let's just look at it."

We walked in, and my princess tiara started to tremble. Please don't get the wrong idea, but when the manager looks and sounds like Deepak Chopra's (for whom I have great respect) eleventh first cousin, I positively knew I wanted to stay at the Hampton Inn. Deepak's cousin said, "The only room with a river view is a smoking room, but if it smells bad, I will spray it." I can feel my lungs quiver and blacken at the thought. We take the elevator to the third floor to look at (and smell) the room. It was the kind of elevator that had an unfinished back wall. I could see the concrete bricks as we moved from floor to floor. We arrived at the third floor. I swear there was incense burning in the hall. We opened the door to the room, and I was overwhelmed with the color brown and the stale smell of tobacco. The moment of truth had arrived!

T-Rex grumbled the unthinkable. "What do you think of the room?"

I know this is a trick question, but the trick is to answer it by being true to myself—and to avoid a confrontation the size of WWIII. It is clearly T-Rex versus the allies, and the allies are all Jewish princesses.

I straighten my invisible tiara and say, "Why don't I call the Hampton Inn and see if they have a nonsmoking room?" I call, they do, it's more money, I offer to pay, he won't hear of it. T-Rex, after all, is a gentleman. I then get the ten-minute-ranting dialogue about how many of these kinds of rooms he's stayed in before he met me and how much he loves to stay in these kinds of places, and how when he travels alone, he stays in these places all the time. Well, good for him, who was obviously raised by wolves.

I hold my ground, practice my yoga breathing and get ready for the rest of the onslaught.

Unbelievably, he says, "Do you want to go to the Hampton Inn?" Duh! I say, "Yes," pick up my things, walk out of the lobby, and leave him to deal with a very angry and insulted motel manager, whose cousin probably will keep me on hold an extra forty-five minutes the next time I call for computer technical assistance.

T-Rex is not speaking to me. We drive in silence down the strip to the Hampton Inn. The lobby is bright and airy, and there are shiny red apples in a bowl and freshly baked chocolate chip cookies at the check-in desk.

We check in. T-Rex is still not speaking to me. As we enter our nonsmoking room with brand-new pillowtop beds, he says coyly, "That other room was really awful, wasn't it? And this is really a much nicer room, isn't it?"

"Yes, it is," I reply, and my breath, which I had mostly been holding, returned to normal.

The crisis is over, and I wonder if President Bush might want to use me to talk with the head of the North Korean government.

Our two days in Pigeon Forge included four hours at the outlet mall, two country music shows featuring bluegrass, Elvis, and Jesus, a tram ride 4,000 feet over the local town of Gatlinburg, Farkel-watching, and incredibly great sleeping on our cloudlike beds. We never made it to Dollywood. The traffic just to get into the parking lot looked like the LA freeway, so we headed for the hills—ours, not hers.

On the beautiful ride home, we passed through the tiny towns called Luck and Trust, NC, and even when we were "out of luck," I realized I had both. Luck and trust, because I know that success in life is to be who you are—a T-Rex, a princess, or a Farkel, living a life of your choosing, but only in a nonsmoking room.

Love to you all.

Alexa
Aka Trailer Trash

P.S. May the forest be with you!

October 3, 2006
Can You Keep a Secret?

Maybe you can keep a secret, and we know that Victoria can, but what about the United States government? One of their secrets is now supposedly out in the open, so we signed up for a tour of the once top-secret "hidden bunkers" at the Greenbrier Resort in West, VA.

In case you don't know, the Greenbrier is a luxury resort that was built in the late 1700s. It is majestically beautiful in a white and floral print way, something like the Palm Beach Breakers in Panavision. The old guard reigns here, and the resort still requires a tie and jacket in the main dining room. Among its list of amenities are a ten-lane bowling alley, an indoor swimming pool with a floating fabric ceiling, and a golf course that was a favorite of President Eisenhower. And now about the "bunker."

During the Eisenhower administration and the Cold War, a secret facility was built to house the president and veep and all the president's men in congress in case of a nuclear attack. Some of you may remember the putting-yourself-under-the-desk drills we had at school and the talk of bomb shelters here and there in the late 1950s. President Eisenhower had always been fond of golfing at the Greenbrier, and because of that and its proximity to Washington, DC, the facility was planned to go there. Under the guise of a hotel renovation, the protected substructure was built 720 feet into the hillside under the west wing of the hotel. The secrecy of this location was maintained for more than thirty years, until May 31, 1992, when the *Washington Post* spoiled all the fun and published a story exposing it. Someone snitched!

According to our tour leader, the day after the story was published, the bunker began to be phased out. The tour begins on a bus that takes you to the secret location and entrance. I must admit I would never have known anything was there. The main door was a beat-up-looking thing with straggly hedges around it. It was definitely not an attention-getter. An underground tunnel led us to one of the four entrances, a large steel and concrete door designed to withstand a modest nuclear blast fifteen to thirty miles away, and to prevent radioactive fallout from entering the facility when sealed off. Under those conditions, anyone entering would have to pass through a decontamination area, remove all clothing, submit to a hurricane-force wind shower, and put on a provided new set of new clothing. A giant incinerator would burn the original clothing, and if, in fact, there had been a death in the bunker, the body would be incinerated. The horrors of the Holocaust flashed in my mind, and I wondered how long it would be before the tour ended and I would be above ground in the clean air and daylight.

Included in the facility are forty-four separate locations,

with 153 rooms, making up a total of 112,544 square feet on two levels. We were told that eighty percent of the facility is now used by a large corporation. And those areas would be off-limits. Hmm, my suspicious Scorpio nature began to prickle.

What we did see was a shelter that included hundreds of bunk beds, an operating room, a dental area, generators, chillers, air handlers, air filters, and lots and lots of wiring, plus laundry and storage areas for supplies of food and medications, a cafeteria/kitchen that covers more than 7,500 square feet, and a television repair shop that was part of the cover-up. We were taken into a small meeting room that had a few rows of chairs and a picture of the White House the size of Alaska on the wall. Why? In case there was a real disaster, the president and/or any of the other congressman bunkerites would be able to stand in front of the picture and generate an "all is well" image/message to the American public. So much for "seeing is believing." I call it political photoshop.

Summing up, the bunker is a beige, utilitarian-looking underground city.

I'm impressed with its efficiency and size, if not with its decor. I also don't believe for a moment that the bunker is no longer a secret refuge. My suspicions were supported as I talked to the locals, the shopkeepers, and some waitstaff at the hotel. Everyone who lived in the small town back in the fifties knew about the bunker, but no one spoke of it. Anyone who worked there would be fined and jailed if they did. But the people I spoke with acknowledged that it was difficult in a small town to hide a 25-ton concrete slab door that comes in by rail, especially when the train runs right through the town.

In addition, there's an airport close by with one of the longest runways in the United States. Why? To accommodate big jets like *Air Force One* that land and take off there all the time. During 9/11, Dick Cheney was flown in and stayed in the bunker. Since then, the locals have seen the president and his wife there on several occasions, as well as many national and international dignitaries. Personally, I think the bunker is still very much part of a security program and the public tours are a perfect decoy to keep the secret.

So, now I'm on to their secret but still haven't found out what Victoria's is. Maybe she meets Bush and Cheney in the bunker, and if she does, I hope she can keep them down there for the next two years.

Love to you all.

Alexa
Aka Trailer Trash

Drag Queens in Tennessee
August 12, 2006

Weather-wise, it was our best day yet . . . 60 degrees at 9:00 a.m., clear, denim blue skies, and a butterfly wing breeze. This was a perfect motorcycle day, so we donned our leathers, boots, and helmets and met up with four local Harley riders (whose names I still don't know) and headed over to Tennessee. The ride took us past picture-perfect pastures filled with rolls of hay covered in protective white vinyl. From a distance, they looked like fields of white marshmallows or mozzarella cheese balls. We stopped at Exit 23 for breakfast at Clarence's, the local Sunday brunch favorite. I could smell the biscuits and sausage gravy from the highway. This country staple is what I call heart attack in a bowl and is accompanied by pancakes with ice cream–scoop sizes of Country Crock imitation butter. They didn't have real butter, skim milk, or whole wheat toast, but I've given up on healthy food.

I hadn't been curious enough to ask where we were going since the day was so beautiful. Just being outside was enough. The "men" started talking about Bristol, Tennessee, home of the NASCAR races, and I knew that "enough" had just changed into something I had never seen or heard. We were heading for the Bristol Dragway at the NASCAR track to see the national motorcycle drag races. *Okay*, I thought. *This will be something to write home about* . . . And I wasn't wrong.

As we thundered along the Tennessee Ernie Ford Parkway, motorcycles were everywhere, their riders and passengers eager to see world championship dragsters. The price of the entrance ticket was $25.00 a person, and hundreds of bikers lined up at the gate to pay. The sun shines hotter in Tennessee, and the temperature became a very uncomfortable ninety degrees, which led to many shirtless men. But more about them in a moment.

The event began with the singing of the "Star-Spangled Banner." The vocalist must have been eliminated from the country version of *American Idol*, but she twanged her way through the high notes, and there was not a cough, sneeze, whisper, or pop-top sound in the place. In the quiet, I observed a sea of leather-vested men with their hands resting over their hearts, standing at attention, and paying tribute to our country and flag. I truly loved their patriotism and admired their respect for the moment. Then, over the loudspeaker, the first pair of dragsters was announced! The moment was definitely over.

Bless their pea-pickin' hearts, those suckers were loud as they roared toward the starting line.

This is a televised event, and the racers are suited up in colors and outfits that resemble Spider-Man. Before they start, they spin their tires to heat up the rubber and increase the traction. They assume the position, which is hugging the front of their bikes and lying down on them to keep the wind resistance to a minimum. It is the Kama Sutra of dragster queens. The colorful bikes have brilliant custom paint jobs, and their engines create a noise level that would—and did—shatter many a beer bottle. Each bike has a wheelie attached to the back—a specially designed roll bar to prevent the bike from flipping over backwards.

The starting lights go green, and the bikes race a quarter mile down a straight track. The deafening decibels of noise can rival any rock concert or powerboat race, so I stuffed enough tissue in my ears to boost Kimberly-Clark's stock for a year. The racers are impressive, as two by two, they barrel down the track, fueled by nitromethane (rocket fuel), spewing fumes the size of a nuclear explosion. Imagine seeing, hearing, and smelling a motorcycle go 215 mph in six and a half seconds. After a few heats, I turned my attention to the crowd. And now the rest of my observations . . .

Most of the onlookers were Harley riders, and their black and orange (Harley colors) T-shirts and caps spoke well for the fabulous marketing job Harley Davidson did. The men outnumbered the women twenty to one, but I wouldn't get too excited about the dating prospects unless you are into tattoos, ponytails, and a lack of dental work.

T-Rex started looking more like Mr. Universe with every second. On a fashion note, the amount of embroidered leather vests did set the tone for fall, but only if embellished with the following sayings: "The Southern sons of Kentucky,"; "The Peacemakers"; "The Prayer Team"; "The Outlaws"; "You are not forgotten, POWs"; and "Valley Desperados." There wasn't one mention of the "Bagel Bad Boys" or the "Gefilte Fish Gang," but remember, we are in the Bible Belt. My two favorite T-shirts were printed with "First in, last out, firefighters rescue," and the overall winner, "Contrary to popular belief, this cross is not a fashion accessory. It's a symbol."

Craig spotted a shirtless work of art that was a tattoo on a man's back. It started below the belt line (otherwise known as the great divide) and was of Jesus ascending from the grip of Satan, up a stairway, and into the clouds of Heaven. These men were serious about their religious beliefs, as well as their motorcycles.

It was almost time to go when I spotted the one slogan that really summed up the whole day: "He would have ridden a Harley."

On the two-hour ride home, I speculated on the identity of who He might be. Based on my ethnic origins and that area, I concluded that He had to be Jesus, not Moses, because no Jewish mother I know would've let her son ride, or God forbid, race a motorcycle.

Love to you all.

Alexa
Aka Trailer Trash

P.S. "Forbidden fruit leads to a lot of bad jams." From the Bible, and a book by Katherine Compton and David Compton, and a lot of roadside signs on churches. Peanut butter gets no mention.

2007

Put Your Dreams in Motion!
(Whatever They Are)
July 2007

Maybe you haven't given one second of thought to Alexa's Trailer Trash adventures. Maybe you haven't even noticed that she's still in Miami and your email inbox is not being bombarded with travel tales from the blue roads of America. And why don't I write during the non-summer months? I guess life gets in the way—not to mention root canals, income tax, and social obligations. Plus, I'm still trying to figure out why I have to press one for English.

But I'm almost ready. That old familiar "get me outta here" feeling is creeping up on me, just like ivy on a vine. And soon I'll be all covered up with the lure of an unknown black taffeta road with a bright white line taking me away from here.

The whole idea is an adventure! For me, it's to experience the discovery on the highways of America and to wake up the craving for adventure that's deep-seated in all of us (well, maybe not all). For some of you, adventure is just getting to the mall on sale day. For others, bungee jumping (G-d forbid), and for others, a day at work is an adventure in itself. But whether it's the waitress refilling saltshakers in a roadhouse in Nevada or a Jewish princess saluting the carved stone heads of presidents in South Dakota, the thrill of each new task and encounter stays with us forever.

The Airstream stands ready to go—shiny and efficient with one new addition. We will have a flock of pink plastic flamingos to grace any tiny landscape where we stop. Well, I never said I wasn't into bad taste, did I? And speaking of Airstreams . . . Did you know that the sixteen-foot Bambi model was on display in the lobby of the New York Museum of Modern Art? Yes, Trailer Trash hit the big city, and when I recently visited, there were plenty of gawkers gathered around the adorable little tin-can traveler.

So, I'm getting ready to roll on, and I hope you'll go along with me and my emails. Right now, the page is blank, but soon, I hope to fill it up with the who, what, and where of this summer's Trailer Trash Chronicles. I look forward to hearing from you. Be safe. Be well. And put those dreams in motion, whatever they are.

Love to you all.

Alexa
Aka Trailer Trash

Run Bunny, Run, Burnsville, NC
July 2007

Am I invisible? I felt like I was because as soon as I crossed the PGA Boulevard, heading north, not one person honked at me, gave me a dirty look, or "the finger." And that continues right up to this minute, four weeks later. And why is that? I'll let you know as soon as I find out, once again, why I have to prove I'm not a robot.

In the meantime, things are really "hopping" in Burnsville. Why, just the other night, we were sitting around my sister's oval oak dining room table. The view is pastoral, full of trees, flowers, and mountains, plus bird feeders. You have to watch with what some call "soft eyes," or you may not see the yellow finch perched on the bright yellow sunflower. And if you look down into your wine glass for just a split second, you'll miss the hummingbirds sipping from the ruby red feeders. And then suddenly, nature creates a moment that interrupts the tranquility of this lovely scene. A bunny rabbit, bigger than a bread box, appeared on the lawn. We watched with intense interest as my sister's dog, a wannabe border collie, spotted the bunny and struck the pose of "I've got you in my sights, rabbit!" (Stop snickering. We don't have cable.) Horrified, we watched, knowing the dog would certainly overtake the rabbit. And then all at once, completely unrehearsed and sounding like a Greek chorus that's been kicked out of the Parthenon, we all started screaming, "Run bunny, run!" I guess you had to be there, but our chorus worked as we watched the white fluffy tail disappear into the deep woods, and the dog turned her attention to a flickering firefly instead. "Run bunny, run!" has now become a family mantra, and we always giggle when we say it, which is often. Simple pleasures rule around here.

And speaking of simple pleasures, Friday nights will find fifty to one hundred of the locals down at the Middle Fork Ridge Lake. They arrive right after work in their beat-up trucks. They park all around the lake with their folding chairs, their Mountain Dew sodas, their families, and they fish for money! How do you fish for money?

Well, it's not like go fish, but it is about catching the right fish—kinda like a fish lottery. The lake is stocked with carp, bass, and catfish. Earlier in the day, a few lucky fish are tagged, and those are the prize-money fish. Everyone pays an entry fee, and the total makes up the prize money, which can be as high as five hundred dollars. It's a most unusual way to spend happy hour, especially in a dry county, but these folks are as happy as you can get. Yup, it's those simple pleasures again. Some people fish for compliments, others for sport, others go to just "set a spell" and be neighborly. It's a "Don't Worry, Be Happy" (song by Bobby McFerrin) pastime. Go fish. Go figure.

You're probably wondering why on earth I'm writing about all of this. I'll tell you. I really love this side of America's culture. I think being around it is like being hit over the head with a two-by-four. Do we really need all that stuff that George Carlin jokes about to be happy when all this "down-home" stuff can be so satisfying? Maybe you like riding in an elevator and not speaking to anyone, or walking through your day with your Bluetooth and Blackberry commanding your time. But right now, it's fun for me to get up close and friendly with some fish folks in an increasingly de-personalized world.

I'm off to Tulsa tomorrow to meet T-Rex.

Love to you all.

Alexa
Aka Trailer Trash

P.S. Did you know that a goldfish has a memory span of three seconds?

My Old Kentucky Home

Horseplay is encouraged here, and the air smells so sweet that we have turned off the AC and are driving with the windows open to take it all in. The rains and delays of yesterday are gone, and the Kentucky bluegrass should be bottled for its delicious natural fragrance and color. The books say that the ancient beds of limestone enrich the grass—making the bones of the horses that graze here especially strong—and sweeten the streams used in the production of prized Kentucky bourbon. Even though we're in the western part of the state, my thoughts turn to the legendary horse, "Man O' War," and a million derby dreams. This is the home state of coal mines, the National Corvette Museum (in Bowling Green), Fort Knox, the Cumberland Gap, the world's longest cave at Mammoth Cave National Park, and the world's largest quilt museum. It's also the birthplace of Abraham Lincoln. He was born in a log cabin in Hodgenville (he lived here until he was two). I had always thought he was born in Springfield, Missouri. So, there you have it . . . Live and learn "with malice toward none and charity for all." Thank you, Mr. Lincoln.

It's very beautiful here—rural gentility, white fences, and

acres of tobacco and wildflowers. Wish we were staying awhile. I'm putting the Kentucky Derby on my list of things I'd love to do next year. In the meantime, we're crossing the Ohio River into Illinois, but only for a few miles as we head for St. Louis. All this, and it's only 10:45 a.m.

Love to you all.

Alexa
Aka Trailer Trash

T-Rex in Tulsa
July 2007

Gordon McCrae and Shirley Jones would've winced, but it was my once-in-a-lifetime opportunity. So, as I landed at Tulsa International Airport, I started singing "Oklahoma." That musical has always been one of my favorites, and although parts of it are a bit dated now, it was wonderful to think of the title song in the actual state where the residents talk about the land and how they belong to it.

Tulsa isn't many people's idea of a good time, nor does it have much to boast about, but I was astonished to find out that it ranks right up there with Miami and New York in Art Deco architecture. And just in case you're a *Jeopardy* watcher, Tulsa is the state with the most Indian tribes. Names like Sapulpa, Okmulgee, and Broken Arrow are everywhere as a reminder of its huge Indian heritage and the thirty-nine sovereign nations. In addition (and this is the pretty one), since the Miss America Pageant started in 1921, Oklahoma has taken the title six times, tying with California and Ohio.

T-Rex was waiting for me in the big red diesel truck. For the past ten days, he'd been training US Air Force pilots on a

Cessna Caravan that would be used in Iraq. My sarcastic self could not resist saying, "No wonder we're losing the war!" But honestly, I'm very proud that he was called on for this, and he loved every minute of it.

All of the pilots were top guns, including a tobacco-chewing lieutenant colonel and captain with nicknames like Snapper and Wheeler. According to Craig, they were all fit, wore Ray-Ban sunglasses, camouflage vests, and boots. T-Rex sported his own special look, wearing a tank top, jeans, and bright-blue Crocs. When he rode up to the airport to meet the guys on his BMW motorcycle, it was love at first sight, despite the forty-year age difference.

We were staying at the Cherry Hill Mobile Home Park, a Trailer Trash oxymoron since ninety percent of the trailers never go anywhere, and if they did, they'd be dragging their string of Christmas lights with them. Plus, there wasn't a cherry tree in sight, but there were a lot of ceramic deer lawn ornaments. Oh well, I repeat, "It ain't home 'til you take the wheels off." With only a day to explore Tulsa, we headed for the aquarium. Others would've spent the day in the Thomas Gilcrease Institute, one of the country's top art museums full of amazing Western art, but remember who I travel with.

I've been to big-city aquariums before, but this one has a horror movie of a shark tunnel, and it's an eerie wonder. As you enter the tunnel, the lights dim, and the rest of the world floats away. You're completely surrounded by plexiglass walls and ceiling, and then the big boys with their jagged tooth smiles swim over and on both sides of you as you walk through. Think silence of the sharks. 'Nuff said.

The riverwalk was next, with boutiques and restaurants along the Arkansas River. Once again, I'm amazed as Middle America shows up with their families, lots of babies, grandparents, and handholding teenagers for concerts in the park. Police patrol the area and will escort away anyone underage who is found drinking. It's all very civilized and almost bland.

As we drive around, we're reminded that the people of Tulsa know they belong to the land. There are signs everywhere on the highways that say "Up with trees," and "Stop the chop." It's a nice city and soon will have something else to boast about. The PGA Tournament is coming to Southern Hills Golf Course. Soon, the tiger (Woods) will join the sharks. Parts of Route 66 and the Santa Fe Trail lie ahead. Tomorrow, we'll cross Oklahoma on our way to Colorado.

Love to you all.

Alexa
Aka Trailer Trash
P.S. "All who wander are not lost." From the Bible verse, Psalm 102:1-4.

The Breakfast Club
July 2007

Good bye, Tulsa and the interstate. It's still early morning, and we've decided to take the road less traveled, or perhaps in this case, the road never traveled. Traveling with Craig is like traveling with Audrey 11, the plant in the "Little Shop of Horrors." He's constantly hungry, and right after breakfast usually asks, "Is it lunchtime yet?"

With no Cracker Barrel or bagel shop in sight, we pull off into the historical town of Pawnee in search of breakfast. As always, when in unfamiliar little towns, we look to see where the most cars or trucks are parked as a sign of a good, popular place. Honest John Fibber seems to be the place, so we park the Airstream and truck—all fifty-five feet of them—right on Main Street. Honest John's looks like the set of an old Western movie. The clientele is all Native American Indian, and we find out that Pawnee is an Indian town, not a reservation, nor would anyone need or want to make a reservation here, if you know what I mean.

But back to Uncle John's . . . The walls are covered with stuffed moose and elk heads, plus skins of wolves, Indian blankets, and one particular plaque that states: "This is the very last moose that roamed the plains of Oklahoma." Now I know why it's called Uncle Fibbers.

After we survived breakfast, I walked out to the trailer and was followed by an Indian named Randi Tiger, a third-generation Pawnee who saw the Airstream and wanted to chat about it. Turned out, he was a firefighter who was one of the crew to go to Texas when the space shuttle crashed about three years ago. And then, just as we were about to pull out, a man in a truck stopped us to welcome us to town and find out how we enjoyed our breakfast. He introduced himself and gave us his card. He's the president of the Pawnee Chamber of Commerce. Just like Miami (not), and so friendly and polite.

Back on Highway 67, we cross the panhandle of Oklahoma. It's not exactly the scenic route unless you're into working oil rigs. We pass them dipping up and down, and they remind me of dinosaurs drinking up large ponds. And by the way, gas is not cheaper here, although I thought it would be. Two hours out of Tulsa, and T-Rex sounds off the names of a never-ending list of airports and Air Force bases he'd used in his training for the top guns. I acknowledge each one with feigned enthusiasm and a "Yes, sir" as I count teepees and taxidermists. It's not the most exciting travel day, but it sure beats crossing Kansas.

Uh-oh. T-Rex cannot find his cell phone. We look everywhere. We stop and go through everything in the truck. Did it fall out at the last gas station men's room? Is it lying in the panhandle dirt where we stopped to check a tie-down on the motorcycle? I call his phone with my phone. Nothing. He tells me he had it on vibrate. Great! My stomach was starting to knot up at the thought of the no-phone outcome, and the reaction that I imagined was coming. I brace myself for the onslaught of a phoneless T-Rex, but there is none. Instead, here's what I hear.

"Oh, well. I can't worry about stuff like that."

What? I know how I would've reacted, but after all, he is a T-Rex, and his ancestors roamed the earth long before Cingular Wireless. Actually, I shouldn't be surprised. I've witnessed this same calm, cool attitude when he broke an arm wrestling in Utah and when the Airstream had three flat tires in the same day crossing from St. Louis to Colorado, and when I imploded the microwave in Branson, MO.

And then he added, "And now I only have to speak to you, Sparkly One." (My nickname.) Oh, yes. A T-Rex can be charming.

We stop for a Blue Bell ice cream, whose slogan is "100 years, and we're still crankin'." Hope we can say the same for all of us someday.

We're pulling into Lamar, Colorado, for the night, and I'll be back in touch soon.

Love to you all.

Alexa
Aka Trailer Trash

P.S. Speaking of phones . . . Only in America do we use answering machines to screen calls and then have call-waiting so we won't miss a call from someone we didn't want to talk to in the first place.

P.P.S. Craig found his phone on the floor in the back seat of the truck, lying beneath six motorcycle jackets and a Snap-on toolbox. Calm, cool, and collected paid off.

Lamar, CO.
August 2007

After eight plus hours in the truck, we stopped at dusk in Lamar, CO, also known as the "mountain branch" of the Santa Fe Trail. There are three motels in Lamar and no RV parks. At this hour, two of the three already have a no vacancy sign, and that's a good thing, because even T-Rex wouldn't have stayed at either one of them. We head for motel #3, the Corn Palace Best Western. Just as we drive into the parking lot, a dusty old car full of Farkels pulls in.

T-Rex looks at me and says, "Run! They're gonna get the last room."

With "Run bunny, run!" resounding in my head, I sprinted to the front desk and whipped out a credit card faster than Gary Cooper's draw in "High Noon." We got the last non-smoking room, and the Farkels got the last room, period.

Lamar is quite unremarkable except for the putrid smell of stockyards right behind the motel and a restaurant called the Hickory House, where they consider pinto beans and rice as vegetables. My good Jewish sport award will surely be waiting for me in Miami.

The next morning, we amble onto Highway 50, aka the Santa Fe Trail. There's little to see here except for acres and acres of irrigated farmlands, feedlots, and cattle ranches. Today I will count silos and cornfields.

You may remember that beginning in the 1820s, and lasting until the railroads were completed, the Santa Fe Trail was the primary link between the United States and the Spanish and Mexican southwest. The trail was established by commercial traders rather than immigrants, and merchants brought manufactured goods by wagon loads, which they exchanged for Mexican silver. My guess is that there were more than a few Jacobsens and Schwartzes making the trek and that the first "oy vey" was spoken by some Jewish pioneer woman. Who could blame her?

At the time of the Civil War, commerce along the trail reached Walmart proportions, with over 5,000 wagons rolling along to Santa Fe. Very little remains of the trail. There are a few almost-invisible stretches of old wagon ruts, and if you take the time to stop, you can stand in the footsteps of those travelers that crossed/schlepped there a century ago. It's still possible to get a powerful sense of what the trail might have been like. Oy vey, indeed!

We continue the drive through Las Animas, the place where Lt. Zebulon Pike had his first glimpse of the rocky peak that now bears his name. This is also the place where Kit Carson died. On to the railroad crossroads of La Junta (meaning the junction), where the open roadside stands are everywhere. We treat ourselves to slices of rock melons and peaches that are sweeter than the ones in South Carolina.

It's finally time to return to the interstate as we approach Denver on I-25. It's a culture shock to go from no traffic and wide-open spaces to the hectic pace of a big city. It's also 90 degrees. Weather is a big part of travel, and we've had days where the temperature varies as much as 40 degrees. Today was one of those days, when just as we passed Idaho City, the Colorado blue sky turned charcoal grey and we were bombarded with hail pellets that bounced off the pavement and the truck. The temperature nosedived to 56 degrees. I felt sorry for the bikers on the road but was secretly glad I was snug in the big red truck.

It was almost dinnertime when we arrived at the River Dance RV Resort (*resort* being a bit of an exaggeration). The silos and cornfields have been replaced by the Roaring Fork River and the Rocky Mountains. Not a bad trade except for the bear alert and the threat of West Nile virus. It's always something.

Love to you all, and even if you're not in a covered wagon, if you're in a rut, there's no time like the present to get out of it.

Alexa
Aka Trailer Trash

P.S. Did you know that there are more chickens than people in the world?

Just Ducky in Aspen
August 2007

First of all, let me say that Aspen is the only town where people pay thousands of dollars to look like they have absolutely nothing. Sort of an anti-cool.

It's the only town around here where you must pay to park, and parking can become an Olympic competition. Trophy wives and fancy cars rule. It's like Palm Beach with mountains, great restaurants, art galleries, people-watching, and the addictive oatmeal raisin cookies at the Paradise Bakery. But today, even the "coolest" of Aspenites turned out for the 14th annual Rubber Ducky Derby.

Imagine the local Rio Grande Park filled with food, games, children, dogs, the Rotary Club, and yellow rubber ducks with sunglasses . . . 25,000 of them sold for $5.00 each. Each duck is given a number, and they're off. The derby is a three-part event, just like the Kentucky Derby. The ducks are launched at precisely the same time, by three dump trucks, into the river. The crowds gather all along the riverbanks and on the bridge, anticipating the race. When the first duck bobs into sight, the crowd goes wild, and then another, and then another until the river is covered with a floating blanket of bath toys.

The squeals of delight from children and adults are deafening. It's hilarious to watch dogs jump into the river and try to get the ducks in their mouths, and the same goes for the little kids. The whole race takes about forty-five minutes, and the finish line finds some serious Rotarians collecting the top fifteen ducks as the winners. These prized ducks are placed in a plexiglass tube and taken to the park for verification on the computer. You would think these men were carrying Fabergé eggs as they march solemnly to their stations. Why is this taken so seriously? Because the winner of the derby gets $1 million. That's right, $1 million. Actually, the odds are a lot better than any lottery. All I could think of was Groucho Marx on his show "You Bet Your Life" and winning a million dollars if you guessed a certain word.

Unfortunately, I could not "duck" the next event of the day . . . going up Independence Pass on the motorcycle. A few years ago, we crossed the pass with the truck, and for some reason, I remember it being a very scary drive, with no railings and deep drop-offs of thousands of feet. I've been successful in avoiding a repetition of that drive ever since.

But today was beautiful, and with the sun shining, I decided to face my fears. We suited up with extra jackets because we were climbing to over 12,000 feet, and it's a lot cooler up there. The first part of the ride wasn't as steep as I remembered, but I had a hard time enjoying it because I was anticipating the next turn, and the next turn, and then before I knew it (actually, it takes about a half hour), we were at the top, and there were only about twenty seconds of the scary heights. We took a picture at the top just to prove my bravery, and then I started to think about how memory and imagination create fears completely out of proportion. What I remembered just wasn't accurate at all. Remember when you were in elementary school and the halls and rooms seemed so big and tall? And then you went back as an adult and you felt like Gulliver in Lilliputian Land? The halls seemed to have shrunk, along with everything else. Well, I thought that might be the reason, but I was already an adult when I made the first drive, and I don't think I've grown any since then, so it's definitely fear building on fear. There's so much we miss because of fear. I'm feeling just ducky that I got to stand on top of a mountain today. Truth is (but don't tell T-Rex), I'd go again.

Love to you all, and good luck facing and conquering your fears.

Alexa
Aka Trailer Trash

These are some of the messages we saw on the marquees of churches on the way to Colorado:

"Too hot for church. What about hell?"

"Life too hot to handle? Come on in. We're prayer-conditioned"

"Tired of religion? Me too. Signed, God."

Taking the Plunge, Glenwood Springs, CO
August 2007

No, I'm not talking about marriage, cleavage, or unstopping the toilet. I'm talking about the hot springs pool in Glenwood Springs, Colorado. I do need to detox from the Big Apple. The horror of spending six hours on an airplane flying back from NYC to Denver is only surpassed by having to put on the leopard print tankini bathing suit I purchased two years ago in the Outer Banks. Fortunately, for my fragile ego, it turns out that the "beautiful people" are not poolside, and my cheesy suit is actually one of the better fashion statements of the day. Cellulite, beer bellies, and tattoos abound, but I don't care, and neither does anyone else. You see, it's all about the water! Using one of the many poolside stair rails, I eased myself in, not knowing how hot the water would feel, and of course T-Rex, the alpha male, just jumped right in, causing a tsunami ripple effect the size of Nebraska. Thank goodness there were no big hairdos to disrupt.

People have been "taking the waters" at the hot springs pool for centuries. The Ute Indians were the first to discover the miraculous healing powers of the hot springs, calling them "yampah," meaning "big medicine." It was considered a sacred place for healing the sick and wounded.

In the late 1800s, mineral water was bottled, and the water was served in the Denver and Rio Grande railroad dining cars. No matter how exquisite the goblets, I'm not sure there's enough alcohol to stifle the pungent sulfur (rotten eggs) aroma for drinking this as a cocktail, but apparently many did.

The practice of using natural mineral water for the treatment or cure of disease is known as "balneology." How's that for a new Scrabble word? Soaking in highly concentrated mineral water is thought to have many health benefits, such as increasing body temperature, thus killing germs and viruses, eliminating toxins, increasing blood flow and circulation, increasing metabolism, and absorption of essential minerals. These are mighty claims, but many have come to the springs to treat their ailments, including Doc Holiday, the famous gunslinger who suffered from tuberculosis. Also, during World War II, the pool was used as a therapeutic tool by physiotherapists in rehabilitating emotionally and physically disabled sailors and Marines.

And now about the pool . . . It claims to be the largest hot springs pool in the world. The therapy pool is 100 feet long and contains 91,000 gallons of water. The temperature is 104 degrees. The large pool is 405 feet long and 100 feet wide. It contains 1,071,000 gallons of water. The temperature is 93 degrees. There are hundreds of people of all nationalities, shapes, ages, and sizes in the pool. For a quarter you can sit in an immersed chair and receive dozens of bubbling hot jets all over your body. It's an instant giggle, and so I did it for fifteen minutes until I felt like overcooked penne pasta. People are advised to stay in the hot pool for only a short time and to drink lots of water (not mineral). I spoke to a young woman who was missing an arm and swears that her aches and pains are relieved every time she takes the plunge, which is about once a month. The pool is open year-round. And what does this wonder water day cost? An all-day basic pass is $17.50 during peak season. That includes use of the showers, lounges, lockers, and an incredible little machine that extracts every last drop of water from your swimsuit—a lot like a salad spinner but for clothes. The hot springs also has a restaurant, water slide, miniature golf, and spa services available. You can spend the entire day there, and we practically did.

How did I feel when it was time to leave? Totally relaxed, body and mind, and a little suntanned as well. I even caught tireless T-Rex yawning, but when I asked him if the day in the hot springs had worn him out, he said, "Oh, no. I'm just stretching my jaw." What is it with these guys?

When the day was over, I hated getting out of the pool and considered that this popular attraction may just be the real Fountain of Youth. Then again, maybe Trailer Trash just needed to make a small splash of her own.

Love to you all.

Alexa
Aka Trailer Trash

P.S. The pool at the Biltmore Hotel in Coral Gables is on my list for this winter.

P.P.S. Did you know that the average woman consumes six pounds of lipstick in her lifetime?

Vortex-Schmortex, Sedona, Arizona
August 2007

So, just what is a vortex? A vortex is a funnel shape created by a whirling fluid or by the motion of spiraling energy. Some familiar examples of vortex shapes are whirlwinds, tornadoes, and water going down a drain. A vortex can be made up of anything that flows, such as wind, water, or electricity.

For years I have heard that Sedona, Arizona, is known as a spiritual power center because of the vortexes of subtle energy located in the area. And for years I've wanted to go there and experience whatever this magical energy had in store for me. T-Rex was willing, so we trailered from Colorado to Arizona. That travelogue will require another story altogether.

Apparently, vortexes are people magnets. Sedona, with a worldwide reputation as a spiritual mecca and global power spot, has drawn healers, movie stars, intuitives, artists, and spiritual guides. I'm in good company! These people come to Mother Nature's Red Rock temples to enrich body and soul. Some explain that the red-orange color of the rocks is one of the most neuro-stimulating colors and enhances creative thinking and problem-solving. In addition, the year-round evergreen vegetation is said to bathe visitors in a sense of hope and renewal, regardless of the season. To top it all off, the spectacular trails and overlooks provide endless opportunities for prayer and meditation.

In a nutshell, the landscape here is about as subtle as an A-bomb, and one would have to be comatose not to be affected by it in some way. Sedona is now in my top five of the most beautiful places I have ever been lucky enough to see. And though I'm not a "religious" person, I do have a great respect for sacredness, and I'm ready to attain a higher spiritual perspective.

I obtain a Sedona vortex map printed in black and white with a description of and directions to each vortex. Some are quite easily accessible—others require a Dave Barry Hunt participant. By now, you've probably guessed that Trailer Trash and T-Rex do not take the road most traveled. Adhering to the no pain, no gain theory, we chose the farthest, most obscure, and most difficult vortex to find.

The Boynton Canyon vortex required driving, hiking, and following Red Rock trail markers in wire barrels. Not soon enough, we arrived at the 50-foot-high knoll. We were told to notice the twisted juniper trees all around this trail, an indication that the energy is strongest at this point. So now we sit, quietly, about thirty feet apart from one another, taking in the desert beauty and waiting for the "rush" that others have described in the presence of the vortex.

T-Rex finally breaks the silence with his usual eloquent speech. "Well? Do you feel anything?"

"Yes," I reply.

He says, "I'm hot, thirsty, and still a little out of breath. What about you?"

"Just hot and thirsty. Oh, better drink your bottled water."

He replies, "Yeah, glad we brought it."

And so, the creativity was already at work. We were speaking to each other in almost complete sentences.

After about forty-five minutes of vortex sitting, during which I worried about finding the pathway back to the motorcycle, we decided that the vortex was just having an off day, or maybe we would have some kind of reaction later.

The only thing I felt later was relief that I hadn't known in advance that this particular vortex was the one that strengthens the masculine/feminine or yin/yang balance. According to the vortex mavens, the "balance" between the masculine and feminine sides is almost as important as growth itself. Now they tell me. If the masculine side strongly outweighs the feminine, you're too strong for the amount of goodness you have, and you tend to do harm because you can be pushy and take unfair advantage of others. On the other hand, if the feminine side greatly outweighs the masculine, you have more goodness than strength, and you tend to let others push you around and take advantage of you.

Emotions are a good indication of this balance. For example, if you feel anger more easily than fear, your masculine side is stronger, and if the opposite is true, your feminine side is stronger. If I had known all this beforehand, I might have had a different perspective on how to take in the vortex experience. For instance, perhaps the thought of scorpions scurrying along the desert pathway would've made me angry instead of fearful, and perhaps T-Rex would've been fearful of flying upside down across the canyon (which he did the very next morning, sans moi!) instead of being angry that the flight didn't last longer. So much for balance.

But maybe it's my imagination or wishful vortex thinking, I have noticed that he is full of kindness, compassion, and patience while I have become more self-confident and risk-taking. Was it the vortex itself, or was it that going through the motions of vortexing had made me aware of things that were already there? I'll never know for sure, but vortex-schmortex, that night, T-Rex insisted on us getting dressed up and going to a five-star restaurant at the magnificent Enchantment Resort. Our table faced out through a huge picture window to a dramatic wall of Red Rock peaks, and as I gazed into my wine swirling down and around in a beautiful crystal goblet, I decided that was all the vortex I needed to be spiritually enriched.

Love to you all.

Alexa
Aka Trailer Trash

P.S. Speaking of sacredness, it is said that when God created the Earth, He/She chose to live in Sedona.

July 26, 2008
Shock and Awe

Murder she wrote. It was in the headlines—the story of this murder that happened two weeks ago. The shocking disregard for human life occurred on the roads of North Carolina. The murderer, a known felon from the state of Florida, shot and killed a North Carolina highway patrolman. The patrolman working in the Asheville area had pulled him over for nothing more than a burned-out taillight. The felon drew his gun and shot twenty-four-year-old David Shawn Blanton Jr. four times. As the officer lay dying, the felon returned to his own vehicle and fled.

What happened next, and continues to happen, shows the contrast between shock and awe in our daily lives. There were truckers close by and en route who saw the incident. They got on their CB radios and put out the word: 10-4. Truckers coming and going in all directions formed a highway blockade in the area, and the felon was arrested in less than fifteen minutes. The helping hands and voices were driving 18-wheelers, sitting high up in their cabs, chewing tobacco, wanting to participate in something good. And they did. Pretty awesome.

year, there won't be a local country road that doesn't see our shadows. It will be a great time for visiting with friends, porch sittin', and lively conversation. Plus, sometimes just being with T-Rex is more adventure than I can handle. So, this year, I'll try to write some stories that capture the little picture in a world where the big picture seems to be hanging by a thread.

Wishing you all a beautiful, safe summer. Please let me know how you're spending yours. Don't forget to write. Don't forget to call.

Love to you all.

Alexa
Aka Trailer Trash

June 14, 2008
Suddenly this Summer!

One of the last people I would have ever compared myself to is the poet, Emily Dickinson. Except for her penchant for wearing white clothing and carrying out friendships by correspondence, the New England recluse and I have nothing in common. But then suddenly this summer, with oil prices approaching levels higher than most people's cholesterol, there is one other comparison that some of you may share, as well. Staying closer to home, aka, the "staycation."

We're not venturing across state lines, and we're finding new ways to entertain ourselves in our own zip codes. Ms. Dickinson, late in life, rarely left her room, yet she was able to write about the world, nature, people, and feelings. I doubt she had a flat-screen TV in there, but I'm sure she had a window. So, suddenly this summer, my window on the world will be a little smaller, but hopefully, none the less bright.

The Airstream may be more of a tree house in North Carolina, where we will make our base camp. It will be the perfect opportunity to explore all the highways and byways that we normally pass on our way to someplace bigger and better. This

2008

The young officer left his wife and infant son. She was shocked and devastated by the loss and suddenly without the means to carry on. Next, it was the bikers who chose to lend a helping hand. A small, simple flyer went out to the local businesses and churches (and we do have a lot them around here) in hopes of getting a small group of riders together who would donate $25.00 to ride in honor of the fallen trooper. All the proceeds would go to the widow. There would be no T-shirt sales and no food vendors to detract from the profits. Just a two-hour, police-escorted ride from Black Mountain to Maggie Valley. The local coordinator, who happened to be a North Carolina state legislator and Harley rider, expected the ride might draw two hundred people.

We read the flyer and decided to go. We showed up early and waited and watched as the motorcycles rode in—hundreds of them, and then thousands of them, lined up for the ride out at noon. Many of them contributed much more than the $25.00, writing checks with tattooed hands, removing their fringed gloves, and reaching deep into leather pouches for large amounts of cash. Generosity, compassion, and respect were given. Shock and awe.

And then the ride began with a backdrop of the Blue Ridge Mountains. The roads were ours. Led by motorcycle police, we thundered along, two by two, past farms, shopping centers, and through major intersections. Traffic was held back at every light to let us roar by. I guess the word had gotten around. Hundreds of people came out on the roads to watch us pass. They brought folding chairs, sat up in the back of their pickup trucks, and waved American flags from the overpasses. Hundreds more stopped in their cars with a thumbs-up, showing respect and compassion—their way of participating.

We rode along in double file, and from the middle of the pack, the red taillights in front of us reminded me of a giant army of red ants. Our slowest part of the ride was around downtown Asheville, where more people were crowded along the sidewalks, and much to my disbelief, were stepping out into the street to touch our hands, holding peace signs, and chanting, "Way to go."

When we reached our destination, a brief memorial service included speeches from some of the local dignitaries, a prayer, and an honor guard salute. The very slender, young, blonde wife stood at the podium, holding her baby, looking out at all of us, incredulous at the number of people—people who never knew her or her husband. We had expected that she would say something, but it became evident that she was frozen with emotion and clearly speechless.

The legislator spoke for her, expressing appreciation and thanking the bikers who "always answer the call." He estimated that the turnout and the money donated had greatly exceeded his wildest hopes. He roughly calculated the number of bikers at 4,500. Pretty awesome. In addition to the bikers, there was another group called the Patriot Guard Riders, whose primary mission is to attend the funeral services of fallen American heroes as invited guests of the family. Their main functions are to show respect for the fallen and to shield the mourning family and friends from interruptions created by any protestors. They also support wounded and injured service members, veterans, and public servants, and coordinate welcome home missions. If you'd like to know more about them, you can go to www.patriotguard.org.

The shock for the family will continue, but so will the awesome reality of what good things people can and will do for one another.

In the meantime, I can barely drive down a country highway without seeing a church marquee designed to attract the spiritually fallen.

For instance:

A new SPF warning: Exposure to the son may prevent burning.

A cool message: Enjoy summer. We're prayer-conditioned.

Driver's education: Don't give the devil a ride. He likes to Drive.

An aviation warning: If God is your co-pilot, swap seats.

An anti-depressant: If you're feeling down, look up!

Love to you all.

Shocked and Awed Alexa
Aka Trailer Trash

2009

September 12, 2009
Whatcha Doin'?

Okay, okay. So I haven't called, and I haven't written all summer. What have I been doing? That's a good question, and depending on your perspective, the answer is either a lot . . . or absolutely nothing.

First of all, after arriving at the house in NC, days are spent cleaning, making beds, and trying to remember where I put everything away last fall. Once settled in, it always becomes a much more domestic lifestyle than in Miami. What do I mean by that? Well, once you realize that the best restaurant in town is the Western Sizzler (a chain known for its abundance of overcooked salty food), cooking becomes a major daily event. Magic Chef doesn't live here, so cooking also involves grocery shopping and cleaning up. Plus, there is usually company for dinner—because a person can only stomach so much of the all-you-can-eat buffet at the WS.

Then we have laundry. Even though nobody notices what you're wearing and probably cares less, after wearing the same T-shirt and jeans for two days, into the wash they go, need it or not. Believe me when I tell you that I have seen men at the gym in denim overalls and black socks.

Of course, I do eat out, which makes the gym a real necessity in order to sustain any semblance of non-life-threatening levels of cholesterol and weight. It's a must in the face of genuine country cuisine that includes biscuits and gravy, homemade fudge, sweet tea by the gallon, and a lot of sittin'. Please remember, this is an area where skim milk is considered an exotic food and folks think spaghetti is a vegetable.

So, now that all the chores are done, I have to choose which activity I'm going to participate in or attend. Since this area has more artists and musicians per capita than any other in North Carolina, I can go to concerts, craft shows, and galleries 24/7. I've seen and heard everything from fiddling and spoon-playing to symphonies and Shakespeare. Plus, every kind of potter, weaver, painter, and glass-blower resides here.

And then there are all the alternative-lifestyle people who believe that their spirit guides have directed them to this area for the right reasons. We call this Asheville's "weird factor," and it often works its way up to Burnsville. Anyone can enroll in the Appalachian School of Holistic Herbalism and learn about the intuition of plants, or study psychotherapy for life transitions and mindfulness, or partake in every kind of massage therapy, colon cleansing, or angel touch energy healing. You can get your hair colored organically, hang out with horses for a better understanding of relationships, or spend the night under the stars learning the correct protocol for extraterrestrial contact. (I'm not making this up.)

As you can see from this diverse list, I'm already pressed for time. I'll have to admit to not having gotten through the list of best-sellers I promised myself I would read, nor have I worked on my golf game. But I have made time to observe and enjoy my surroundings, this even without the help of the psychology of mindfulness. I agree with a friend who says, when you come up here, an invisible veil comes down between you and the problems of the world. Maybe it's the quiet, maybe the lack of city stimulus sounds and sights, maybe it's the kind and friendly ways of the local people, or maybe it really is the mountain vortex and the spirit guides.

All I know is, it feels like being in a yoga class all summer, breathing, stretching, relaxing, and letting go of all the crap to let in all the real good stuff. I smile and get a major kick out of the fact that the hostas (also known as plantain lilies) I planted three months ago have grown green and strong. I think it's really remarkable that a tiny little hummingbird found its way to my porch and sips delicately from my feeder. I notice every degree change of temperature because I'm not living in an air-conditioned box. I don't feel fearful. I don't lock my house during the day and rarely lock my car at all. And I'm not suspicious if a stranger says hello—and most do. But I really must sign off now because the Carolina Mountain Literary Festival is here, the Saturday flea markets are all over the place, there's a car show in the Sav-More parking lot, and the Humane Society is having an adoption day near the CVS. And yes, I am having company for dinner.

Please tell me what you did or didn't do this summer. I hope it was wonderful.

Love to you all. I'll see you sometime in October.

Alexa
Aka Trailer Trash

April 23, 2009
Rhapsody in Blue

The call came last week. The RV that T-Rex ordered three months ago is ready. That's the good news for him. The bad news for me is that we will have to drive the truck 1,500 miles to Elkhart, Indiana, to pick it up. Please understand that T-Rex is a man who regularly gets excited about something as mundane as breakfast, so this purchase was his ultimate "stimulus" package. He has always wanted what I was soon to nickname "the beast," and enthusiasm was bubbling up in him like Old Faithful. I, on the other hand, was still feeling nostalgic about seeing the Airstream sold. Mars and Venus, here we go again.

The big red truck was loaded with barely breathing room for a flea. One quick stop, and I would've been knocked unconscious by a toaster oven. But we would have to move everything that had been in the Airstream into the new beast. Plus, I wasn't sure about shopping opportunities in Elkhart, currently the unemployment capital of the United States. I'm not a morning person, and we left at 6:00 a.m. By the time we had driven through Florida, Georgia, and half of North Carolina, I wasn't an afternoon or evening person, either. But enough about me...

About an hour before we stopped for the night in Charlotte,

NC, T-Rex informed me that the following day we would have to get up extra early because we would be making a stop in Summersville, West Virginia. This stop would take us out of the way, but he was going to have his motorcycle lift removed from the bed of the truck and sold to a man named Roger McKinney. Bleary-eyed as I was before dawn, I must admit that West Virginia, the Mountain State, is absolutely beautiful—rolling and rural. We arrived in Summersville, and by some miracle, met Roger in the appointed spot, right in front of Between the Buns hamburger joint that had a great view of the mobile homes across the road.

I've always thought T-Rex lived in the bachelor "house of horror" until we stopped at the McKinneys'. It was time to stretch my legs and use the bathroom, and I ventured to the front door while the men sized up the task at hand. Before I could get to the front door, the garage door came flying open, and there she was, the Mrs., offering me use of the facility and a tour of her hand-built home. I accepted, and that's when I met Ramona, the talking parrot.

Wanda (aka the Mrs.), while covering her mouth with her hand, was proud to tell me that the parrot had free run of the house and even showers with her. She said, "Why, this morning, he was eating peanut butter off the tray table and watching TV with me."

In about three minutes, Wanda told me that their previous house had burned down and Roger had built this one by hand. Then she told me about her quadruple bypass surgery and pulled open her snap-front housecoat to show me that the "scars hadn't healed just yet."

My averted eyes scanned the living room littered with parrot feathers, Walmart bags, and Mountain Dew soda cans as I tried to find the nearest graceful exit. Just as I was about to say my goodbyes, Wanda apologized for not "having my uppers in" and was interrupted by blood-curdling laughter. It was Ramona. When I commented on the sound, Wanda started to laugh, and then I knew that a sequel to *Mommy Dearest* could surely be filmed in this house.

She followed me out laughing and telling me that she stays home from work now because Roger doesn't have a driver's license. I didn't want to ask why. As we stood at the top of their 28-acre ramshackle paradise, three deer ran across the meadow in between the propane tanks and the abandoned trailers. The air was damp and misty, and a certain serenity prevailed. I felt sure that these people were every bit as happy as anyone I know . . . toothless and all.

Removing the motorcycle lift was too much for Craig and lost-driver's-license Roger, so they called in a helper with a forklift. It was hard to have a conversation with either of "'em ole boys" because they had been working since 4:00 a.m. to build stalls for $200,000 show horses. And I think they drank a bit to keep it going . . .

I had been sitting in the truck, hoping this would be over soon, and finally it was. Just like Wanda's teeth, the lift was finally out. We were about to turn out of their driveway when Wanda came out of the house laughing that spine-tingling laugh and ran up to my side of the truck. I rolled the window down, and she smiled without covering her mouth.

"I just wanted to show you my store-boughts."

What could I say, except, "You look beautiful."

For a poster woman for Dunkin Donuts, she did.

To make a long story short, we arrived in Indiana and fell in love at first sight with the big blue, black, and grey, 36-foot fifth-wheel trailer. We stayed overnight in the RV dealer's parking lot and tried all the systems, used the washer/dryer, slept in the king-size bed, and had to spend two full days in ground school to learn about every switch and hose.

Fickle princess that I am, the Airstream is now a faint, fond memory, and "the beast" has completely captivated me. It is beautiful, and whoever said that size doesn't matter must have been talking about something else. T-Rex is overjoyed with his new possession and cannot wait to take it on the road back to Miami. But first, we must find our way around Elkhart.

Indiana is the Hoosier State, and in spite of that, no one in Indiana knows what a Hoosier is. Everyone I asked just shrugged their shoulders and said they weren't sure, so I resorted to Google. Even Google was vague, but a likely possibility is an alliteration of *hoozer*, an English-dialect word recorded in Cumberland, England, for big, burly, uncouth frontiersman. Something like Indianans, I guess. Turns out that Hoosier was just one of a variety of disparaging terms used to describe the inhabitants of certain states. For example, Texans were called beef-heads, Alabamans were called lizards, and Nebraskans were called bug-eaters. North Carolina Tar Heels is one of a few that stuck, and their nickname has survived as a sports team. Them's fighting words, but only on the playing fields. Florida (always a state of confusion) might be called Hoosier Daddy State, and certainly, we've been called worse. Turns out that Elkhart is not a city that has much going for it. The best restaurant in town is a 24-hour diner called Callahan's, and the best store is JC Penney. Time to hook up the beast and head south.

No matter what you may think of Walmart, they have a policy that suits RVers. You and your rig can spend the night in a Walmart parking lot for free all over the United States. And so, we pulled the beast into a Berea, Kentucky, Walmart Supercenter, which is open twenty-four hours. After ten hours on the road, we found a perfect spot along the parking lot perimeter, turned on the generator, and slept among the truckers and shoppers. I thought I had hit rock bottom with this overnighter, but there are perks. First of all, regardless of how you look or how much you weigh, you will always be the thinnest person in a Berea Walmart. And yes, you'll probably have the best teeth. Besides, who wouldn't sleep peacefully knowing that all the Oreos you could ever want were just footsteps away?

We hope you will come by and see the big blue beast. It's really a beauty!

Love to you all.

Alexa
(Aka Not So Trailer Trashy)

Have Pungi, Will Travel
June 2, 2011

Some people are afraid of everything. That may be hard to understand for some of you alpha types. Some people limit their fears to finances, health, and relationships—understandable for most. Some people fear the dentist, a speeding ticket, or a final exam. Count me in.

And then there are the universal and totally acceptable fears for us city dwellers that include rodents, spiders, and the king of all completely rational fears . . . snakes.

Why am I bringing this up as I sit in the dentist's office in Miami (not completely unafraid)? And may I add, with not a snake within striking distance for miles? Because in about two days, I will exit the glories of this city's overpriced parking, condo glut, and sushi restaurants and once again head for my summer retreat—Burnsville, North Carolina.

The advance team has been summoned. I've been assured that all is well up there. My cabin has been cleaned. The rocking chairs are on the porch. The cable TV is on. The toilets flush (yes, there is indoor plumbing), and the water heater is working. Now all I have to do is throw everything I own into my small car and drive thirteen hours. But the phone rings...

It's Craig (aka T-Rex), part of the advance team. He's calling from my porch. "There's been a little excitement here."

"Oh really? What?" I asked, thinking that perhaps one of the neighbor's cows got loose again.

Nope, not that lucky. It seems that while the "boys" were in the carport, they found a long piece of black rubber coiled up next to my garbage can. Turns out it was a seven-foot black snake. Turns out it was very angry when the boys tried to whisk it away with a broom, practically snapping the bristles in half.

So, I asked, "Did you kill it?"

"No, we just chased it into the woods."

"Why didn't you just kill it?"

"Well, it wasn't hurting anything."

This empathetic reply, from a retired North Miami police officer and a commercial jet pilot, both of whom wouldn't think of taking out the garbage unarmed.

Oy vey. Now I have to worry that the angry snake will be having a family reunion back at my cabin. What's a princess to do? No problem. In addition to the mini food chopper, the Waterpik, the Bed Bath & Beyond coupons, and the entire contents of my apartment already packed in the car, I'll add the following: a white turban, a necklace made of shells and beads, my longest dangling earrings, a flutelike instrument called a pungi, a round basket, and my greatest fears. Cause I've discovered, if you can't kill it, then perhaps you can charm it.

Wish me luck, and I'm wishing you all a happy, healthy, and adventurous summer. Please keep in touch, and so will I.

Love to you all.

Alexa
Aka Trailer Trash

Roll Me Over, and Do It Again
July 2009

I bet while you were sipping your café latte, you didn't know that all-girl roller derbies are popping up all over the country. Just like a groundhog, one has popped up in Asheville. So, we just had to go and witness "the red, white, and bruised" Blue Ridge Roller Girls bout against the Low Country High Rollers. Talk about girls' night out!

It reminded me of a wild and crazy *Saturday Night Live* parody of traditional roller derbies (about which I know nothing but can only guess would be a bit more professional). What I saw was a blur of women on roller skates, whizzing around a small circle over and over again. The action gives new meaning to "dizzy blonde," and just watching them can cause instant vertigo.

Roller Derby 101 involves two teams, each made up of a pivot, a jammer, three blockers, and the pack. The jammer is the point-scoring player who starts twenty feet behind the rear of the pack. She has to skate through the entire pack one time and lap the pack before she can begin to score points. It's easy to see why this sport is natural for women. Imagine push-and-shove sale day at Bloomingdales. Everything is seventy-five percent off until noon, and the doors open at 9:00 a.m. Get the picture?

Aside from an overload of the killer instinct, these girls have something else going for them—risqué uniforms and raunchy nicknames. They wear black push-up bustiers, hot pants so short they could double as tube tops, and colorful fishnets that would make a grouper blush. I tried to follow the game but had more fun reading the wickedly creative names on their tiny tops: B.Elsie Bubb, Sofonda Givenstitches, Rigor Morticia, and the home favorite: Mazel Tov Cocktail. Even the refs get into it, like Forrest Ump.

The rules state that illegal maneuvers include grabbing, tripping, kicking, pushing, punching, and holding, and so everyone tries to grab, trip, kick, push, and punch as often as possible. This sport involves a lot of falling down and getting up, and probably a serious death wish. This is the only sport I know of that brings together the love of roller skating, fierce competition, brawling, lipstick melodrama, and a need for full-coverage health and life insurance. But it is the perfect sport for an athletic drama queen who wants to forget about her day job. Some of these women are teaching our children spelling.

And now, as if Roller Derby karma and I were one, the Drew Barrymore movie *Whip It* is coming to a theater near you. I'm not going to be a Roller Derby princess anytime soon, but with any luck, the pillow-fighting competition will be in town before I leave.

In the meantime, I'm going to check my brains at the door of the local flick video and rent *Kansas City Bomber* (1972), starring Raquel Welch. I'll enjoy this guilty pleasure while folding the laundry.

Love to you all.
Alexa
Aka Not as Trashy as the Derby Girls

Frolicking with the Oldies
December 30, 2009

Diesel sounds. That's the first thing I notice as we drive into the KOA RV park in Okeechobee. What am I doing here? Well, since I don't know who Lady Gaga is and have no desire to spend $500.00 at the Fontainebleau Hotel on New Year's Eve to find out, I'll be frolicking with the oldies instead.

Most of the "folks" in this park come from places that are really cold: Maine, New Jersey, Michigan, and Ontario are just a few of the license plates I've seen already. They stay several months and live in their "rigs" full-time. Big-rig trailers, as opposed to motor homes, need to be pulled by trucks, and most of those trucks are diesel. Why? The men know, and the women don't care, as long as they get where they're going.

But the sound of a diesel truck is undeniable. It's somewhere between an offshore powerboat engine and an elephant with a bad case of bronchitis. Other than that, the silence here is refreshing.

If any of you have ever doubled over with laughter while listening to Jackie Mason's routine about the difference between the Jews and the Gentiles, then you'll appreciate what happened next.

When we checked in, we were assigned space #5. Now, try to visualize parking a 37-foot, 13.5 feet tall, 16,000-pound piece of rectangular metal on a concrete slab the size of a drainboard. This is not a walk in the park (pun intended), but T-Rex could put the beast on a Post-It Note if he had to. Now, add to the challenge that the beast has to be backed in. And so, he begins, lining it up, going forward, backing up, forward again, turn a little to the right, a little to the left . . . perfect, and he's there. All the men in the neighboring spaces are watching, hoping to be asked to help, and all the women just watch in wonderment, silently thinking that childbirth was easier.

After several minutes, the beast is perfectly situated, and there are several thumbs-ups and even more people saying, "Nice job." And then T-Rex makes the first fatal mistake of the day, a la Jackie Mason's routine. He asks me, the princess, if I like the space. He thought it was just fine. Do I like the space? What's to like? It's 48 degrees here today, and this space has no sun in the middle of the day. It's backed up to an unattractive chain-link fence, and there's a yapping dog in the site next to ours, plus a big bush that blocks the view of anything that might be attractive.

So, I remain silent. In this instance, silence means displeasure, and so T-Rex made his second fatal mistake. He asked me if I wanted to move. Move? I didn't want to be in this space to begin with. So, of course, I did, but after witnessing the Olympic gold medal backing-in event, I hesitated, and that's when T-Rex made his third fatal mistake.

He said, "Should I go to the office and see what other spaces are available?"

Confucius said, "He who hesitates is lost."

So, I said yes.

After getting a list of seven available spaces, we drove around in my car to see which space I liked best. The pressure was on, as I was thinking about being seated in a restaurant, the disadvantages of certain tables—too drafty, too near the bathrooms, too dark, too bright, too near the kitchen. And you know that "we people" never accept the first table we're given. We finally settled on space #55. It's near the clubhouse, sunny all day, has nicer neighbors, and a beautiful tree offers just the right amount of shade. And then T-Rex had to pull out of space #5 and into #55 and amaze the onlookers all over again. I'm willing to bet that none of them ever moved from an assigned space once they were in it, and most of them never heard the Jackie Mason routine, either.

Finally, we settled in, hooked up, and it was time to go grocery shopping. That's when I knew I was out of Miami and Dade County. Little old Okeechobee has three markets: Publix, Winn Dixie, and a Super Walmart.

T-Rex asked, "Where do you want to shop?"

Are you kidding? After having my way with the space selection, the least I could do was let him pick the grocery store. He chose Winn Dixie. I would've picked Publix. So, what else is new?

Unlike shopping at home, when I asked where something was in the produce department, a polite young man walked me to the exact spot, and in perfect English, offered to pick out some "good eatin'" pears and a ready-to-eat cantaloupe. When we checked out and paid, the cashier asked if we had a Winn Dixie card. We didn't, so she gave us one and told us we would save $10.00. She handed us the cash and apologized for not asking us sooner. Just like Miami!

Next, I bought our tickets for the New Year's Eve bash at the park. Beverly was in charge of the sales, and I found her in the mail room (a hotbed of excitement) playing a game of cards called hand and foot. She assured me that this year's party would be better than ever, with a live band, a buffet of hors d'oeuvres, noisemakers, decorations, and a cash bar (all drinks, $3.00). The cost of the ticket per person is $2.00, and Lady Gaga is drifting farther and farther away from my mind.

I may write again before we leave, but if I don't, it's because I'm practicing the electric slide and walking around the park just to make sure there isn't another space I like better. The women will understand, and the men don't care.

Here's wishing you all a happy & healthy New Year . . . and a perfect table, not near the toilets, next time you go out for dinner.

Much love.

Alexa
Aka Trailer Trash

2011

Rusty and Edna
June 13, 2011

Question: Why is it fun to stay in an RV park?

Answers: You can be close to nature, and it's cheap. You get to see your neighbors sit around all day and do absolutely nothing, and if you don't like it, you can unhook everything and leave in less than ten minutes.

Now, about the neighbors. In RV lingo, there are full-timers and part-timers. Full-timers are the people who live in mobile homes (the ultimate oxymoron 'cause they never go anywhere). Part-timers are the people who travel from place to place for months at a time but still keep another residence. The last, a yet-to-be-described category, I call old-timers.

Let me tell you about one of the neighbors in the Boone Hill RV Park in Burnsville. Henry is a part-timer who was arrested for a DUI while driving his tractor on the highway in Florida. When the state trooper pulled him over, he had a plastic cup full of vodka in the drink holder attached up near the steering wheel. Henry's driver's license no longer exists, and he does his drinking closer to home . . . right next door. That brings me to Edna and Rusty.

The luck of the draw put T-Rex and his RV right next to Edna and Rusty's trailer. At first glance, this couple looks like full-timers because they have a nifty little wooden porch attached to the front of their trailer, some flowering plants, and a clothesline hung along the side. After several pleasantries and the usual neighborly scanning of one another, we actually have a conversation. They are both originally from Burnsville, and that immediately makes their speech almost unintelligible. They twang through their life stories, and Edna does most of the talking because Rusty can barely get a word out between inhaling cigarettes. Edna gives me their complete medical history, which includes the fact that Rusty had a stent put in last year and the doctor warned him if he kept smoking, he'd be back for another one.

Rusty doesn't give a damn, and he's clearly addicted to the nicotine. His complexion is the color of his ashes, and his hair, which is also ashen, belies his name. His one outstanding feature is his eye color—bright turquoise blue, the color of the waters in The Bahamas. I asked Edna if that was what attracted her to him, and she evaded the question but answered with, "We will be married fifty years next May."

Rusty looked up through his smoke rings to interject. "You better plan on celebrating without me, 'cause I don't think I'll be around."

Edna's eyes are blue, too, but paler, and they rolled up and around as if to dismiss the possibility. More of their life story revealed two sons, four grandchildren, his career as a prison guard, and hers as a van driver for a nursing home. They've traveled all over the United States in their RV but are now splitting their time between summer in Burnsville and winter near Orlando, FL.

We got the grand tour of their trailer and an offer of homemade cornbread. FYI, Rusty is proud that he keeps his loaded .38 on site, which brings me to another neighbor, although he only stayed for one night.

This was a young man who rode into the park on his motorcycle. It was just about twilight time, and he wanted to pitch his tent and stay over. The owner of the park was skeptical. He'd had a bad experience awhile back with a biker, but T-Rex intervened with a small white lie about this being a friend of his and got the okay for him to stay. The young man had a Hennessy hammock and expertly tied it between two posts near Edna and Rusty's trailer. I could see Rusty's turquoise-blue eyes fixed on the stranger. All those years at the prison made him less than trusting.

The hammock is a fascinating contraption. It looks like a banana with a Velcro closure, allowing one occupant to slide in and then seal himself inside against insects and rain. I'm impressed but not tempted to trade this for my king-size Sleep Number mattress and AC.

T-Rex offered the young man a beer, and he sat with us and chatted for quite a while. He manages a golf course in the nearby town of Boone. He's thirty-seven, has a wife, and three children—one just a week old. About twice a year, with his wife's blessings, he takes off on his motorcycle to clear his head and see new places. He talked about wanting to go to Lebanon to meet Muslims. We suggested Colorado might be a better choice for scenery and new friendships. Last year, he stayed in a hostel in Harlem and said it was the most satisfying experience of his life.

After a while, our biker friend Fred Peek said good night and headed for town to get some dinner.

By the time I got up the next morning, the hammock and biker were already gone.

T-Rex returned from his breakfast with the "local boys," and with his usual enthusiasm, came charging into the trailer waving a piece of paper. "Wait 'til you read this."

It was a hand-printed note from Fred Peek, written on the backside of a flyer from the Christian Fellowship. I thought it was worth sharing with you in its entirety.

Dear Craig,

It was a great pleasure meeting you. I could have talked with the two of you for hours. Thanks for the cold beer and your time. I pray that you both would have a good full life & above all else, that you would know what is the length, the width, the depth, and the height of God's love for you. Thanks again. You're a kind man.

If you're in town and would like to play golf or even ride bikes— Fred Peek (phone number).

Now, it was my turn to run next door and show this letter to Edna and Rusty. I had to read it to them because they couldn't find their glasses (or maybe they were embarrassed at being uneducated), but after I finished reading it, I think I heard a "Well, I'll be damned" from suspicious old-timer, Rusty.

And for me that morning, the fun of staying in an RV park was seeing a retired prison guard let his guard down.

Love to you all.

Alexa
Aka Trailer Trash

P.S. Latest church slogan seen: "If you're looking for a lifeguard, ours walks on water."

2015

The Ark Encounter (as in Noah's), October 2018

It's been raining a lot this summer in North Carolina. We've had flash floods, rivers overflowing, mudslides, and more umbrella days than not. That said, I made the colossal mistake of mentioning that now would be a great time for an ark. Just a reminder, North Carolina is in the Bible Belt, and Burnsville is probably the buckle, so I shouldn't have been surprised when someone nearby said, "But there is an ark in Williamstown, Kentucky." My innate desire for some weirdness and a small getaway kicked in immediately.

After calculating the five-hour drive that would take us from Burnsville through Tennessee to Kentucky, T-Rex couldn't pack his overnight bag fast enough. What to wear to an ark? I figured that almost anything, including a toga, would be appropriate garb, so I quickly followed suit (no pun intended) and was ready to go. We planned a one-night stay, left the RV behind, and hit the road in the Alfa Romeo Giulia.

We arrived at Williamstown, which I'm sure was a minus-zero town until the ark was built there two and a half years ago. I had put my five hours in the car to good use looking up ark-encounter factoids. We wanted to be prepared for the main attraction. Just the facts here: it's the largest wooden structure in the world. It's 510 feet long (that's a football field and a half). The ark is 85 feet wide and 51 feet high.

The idea for this ark came from an Australian-born man named Ken Ham (already far from Kosher). He believes that the Book of Genesis is historical fact and that the universe is approximately 6,000 years old. He disbelieves the theory of evolution and blames the idea of it on present-day cultural decay. So much for self-evolving, and now I have to worry about serpents, too!

We drove from our motel to the theme park early the next morning and found throngs of people already in line to buy tickets. In the distance, the ark was still obscured by the early morning fog, so we boarded the shuttle bus that would take us to see it up close and personal. After about five minutes on the bus, the fog started to lift, and there was a universal gasp from fellow passengers as the ark came into view. Despite my research, nothing could have prepared us for the massive size and craftsmanship of this structure. It absolutely filled the sky and the ground. Yes, in this case, size does matter.

I approached the ark entrance with my usual irreverent attitude. I do enjoy the stories of the Bible, but I'm not much of a believer. Just as I was thinking, "What's a nice Jewish girl doing in an ark like this," T-Rex, aka the fashion police, directed my gaze to two beautifully dressed women in plus-size T-shirts. The first tee had an image of a big cross and the words "Not today, Satan." The second woman's bright yellow tee was emblazoned with "I was raised on sweet tea and Jesus." I knew I should've worn the toga.

The line of "believers" is long, but we finally reach the main entrance. This may surprise you, but there were no arks when I was growing up on Miami Beach, so I was very excited to have a new experience.

Up, up, up the beautifully designed ramp, we approached the first of three floors. The first floor is titled "The Flood Begins."

In an excellent attempt to recreate what it might have been like inside an ark, the interior is dimly lit as if with oil lamps. The first vignette we see is a life-size scene of Noah's family praying. The figures are three-dimensional and look very real. The room is filled with woven baskets, colorful jugs, and exotic carpets. It all looks authentic, but what do I know? Next are the hundreds of containers that would have held the grains, oils, spices, and drink staples. Again, the colors and textures of everything look real, even though they're artificial. We continue on to see replicas of the animals brought on board, two by two. The furs and fangs are perfectly portrayed. Unfortunately, this reminds me of Bill Cosby's hysterical comedy routine where he's Noah and the Lord is directing him to build an ark, and he keeps saying, "Right." Well, I guess that ship has sailed. Sorry, Mr. Huxtable. No sex offenders allowed on the ark.

The second level is titled "Technology on the Ark." This includes an explanation of how the food was chosen and stored and how the animals were cared for. Noah would've loved the new technology because this ark has Wi-Fi, video presentations, indoor plumbing, and elevators for those who can't—or don't care to—walk up and down the ramps to each floor. If you're going "arking," please wear comfortable shoes. We estimated it to be about a four-mile walk.

The Bible story continues on the third level, titled "After the Flood." We get to roam through the living quarters of Noah's family. They are quite nicely furnished, making use of hammocks, daybeds, and handwoven wall-hangings. There are tons of informational writings along the corridors. Most of them explain the journey of the ark and emphasize religious teachings. The self-guided tour is concluded by learning the "trustworthiness of the Bible" and its history, and of course, a conveniently directed path back down to the first floor and gift shop. I resisted the key chains with crosses, and the bookmarks with biblical quotes.

I did learn that before the Flood, God intended vegetables and fruits to be the sole diet of man. After the Flood, meat and fowl were allowed, but only after the blood was removed. This sounds like Kosher meat to me, yes? And speaking of animals, there's a small zoo outside the ark, full of exotic animals, including an adorable baby kangaroo that took a fancy to T-Rex. Too bad he won't fit in the Alfa Romeo.

A few other things I had read about the ark during the drive added to my original skepticism. The first is that Noah was said to be 675 years old when he built the ark. Even though he had helpers and was on a strictly vegetarian diet, that's really pushing it. The second is that the exhibits show man and dinosaurs co-existing back in the day. Small children playing with T-Rex's ancestors would've indeed been a miracle. All credibility just vanished.

So, all in all, I was impressed with the ark. It was my first ark, and they say you always remember your first. The ark-itecture is fabulous, the ark-ifacts look authentic. The place is beautifully organized, climate controlled, and immaculately clean. On the way out, we were told that if we had purchased the combo ticket, we could've gone down the road and toured the Creation Museum. Thank God, whoever She is, we decided to skip that. I can only handle so much religion in one day.

Mr. Ham plans to extend the two exhibits into one gigantic biblical theme park. In the meantime, I was thinking that some equal time for the non-Christians might include an ark mitzvah, but just then, my thoughts were interrupted as another triple-X T-shirt came into view. This one stated, "Jesus loves you, but I'm his favorite." That was enough for me and T-Rex. We're outta here.

Love to you all, and please, keep the faith . . . whatever yours is.

Alexa
Aka Trailer Trash

2016

Sometimes the Getaways Get You! January 2016, Coldest Weekend of the Year in Florida

The getaway was planned for several days. We were going to visit friends from NC who spend their winters in Orange City, FL. Like a moth to the flame, the thought of a weekend with low-rise buildings, Spanish moss, and vintage Florida is irresistible to me. I couldn't wait and wished we could get there faster and stay longer. Be careful what you wish for!

As we've done countless times before, we loaded up the beast, packed the essentials, and headed out toward the Florida Turnpike. It was 7:00 a.m.

There actually is no term that begins to describe maneuvering fifty-eight feet of truck and trailer through lanes of Dade County morning commuters. In addition to driving, they are texting, applying makeup (even some of the men), and calling on every ounce of caffeinated aggression to move forward a solid foot. Eventually, we reached the place I always refer to as civilization, which is just north of PGA Blvd. Land and sky become visible, and road rage disappears.

At last, we settle into a good mile-per-hour pace and are

looking forward to our first stop, the Cracker Barrel. I can't help but notice that T-Rex is coughing. When questioned, he quickly answers, "I'm fine."

After a "healthy" breakfast of biscuits, butter, honey, eggs, and fried apples, we get back in the truck for the rest of the four-hour drive.

We arrive at the Orange City RV Park, which I now refer to as the RV park from hell. Yes, even "Trailer Trash" knows a good park from a crappy one. The office person assigns us our space, and we wind around narrow and crowded lanes to find our spot . . . space 263. Why am I not surprised to see that space 263 is already occupied by two 18-wheelers and a storage trailer?

We then have to wind all the way back to the office because the park doesn't have a direct phone line, but rather an 800 number that someone in Chicago answers. Big help. No problem! T-Rex goes for the big bucks and gets us a "premium" space. Yes, they have one. We wind our way around to it, and it's what is called a back-in rather than a pull-through. This normally wouldn't be a problem for T-Rex, who used to haul sixty-foot race boats. He could back up a rig all the way to Texas if he had to. But it had been raining for the past five hours, bringing in the cold front, and the ground was covered in rain-soaked, muddy mulch.

The powerful Dodge Ram 350 diesel doesn't have four-wheel drive. However, T-Rex pulls forward to the open space in front of us and starts to "back in." The Ram makes a sound I've never heard before. It's something like what I imagine a rhinoceros getting a root canal without Novocain would make.

The tires spin and dig in. One more attempt, and it becomes obvious that we will not be backing up without assistance. Just then, Rob, trailer park genius, comes along in his golf cart. He offers to get his buddy, who has a tractor. The tractor buddy miraculously appears, pulls our rig back into the space, and we are finally in position on a concrete slab. All is well inside, but outside the temperatures are dropping. Oh, and did I forget to mention that T-Rex has been coughing for the past five hours in the truck, and now every three minutes since we arrived? He still insists he feels fine, isn't sick, has had this before, and doesn't want a lecture. Oy!

And now more about the "premium space." It affords us the unappealing luxury of being surrounded by French Canadians and their clotheslines—the kind I haven't seen since the 1950s that look like maypoles. Printed swimsuits with skirts and black socks adorn the lines. Plus, they have yapping dogs and souped-up truck engines. And did I mention the extraordinary view and smell we have of the park's dumpsters right across the way? We find out the next morning that the garbage trucks come daily, offering enough noise to drown out the French Canadians' dogs. A true trailer park symphony.

The rain has subsided, and the big chill drops over us like an ice-cold hand. Temperatures continue dropping, and T-Rex continues coughing. My fear of dreadful diseases and dislike for the cold weather have kicked in. Have I died and gone to Hell?

We met our friends and had dinner. T-Rex continues coughing, and I'm trying to stay clear. That's easier said than done in an RV.

The next morning, we wake up to 30 degrees and 30 mile an hour wind. T-Rex is still coughing. I'm very concerned. Is this pneumonia, bronchitis, or some form of trailer park flu? At the risk of starting the next war of the roses, I insist that he go to the ER. When he readily agrees, I'm really worried. We drive to the local hospital, walk in, and they send him in immediately. No four-hour wait. No request for insurance. No one else there. Just like Miami!

He comes out, thumbs-up, diagnosed with a touch of bronchitis, Z-pak, and oral cough syrup prescriptions. Feeling relieved, we fill the scripts, meet our friends for lunch, and for the first time in two days, there is no coughing. Things are looking up until we realize that our beloved friends are Republicans of the Tea Party conservative sort. Regardless of your political preferences, these days, it's clear that friendships can be damaged or destroyed when there are opposing views. I truly love these folks, so I keep my thoughts to myself and enjoy T-Rex's cough-less company.

Orange City reminds me of Miami forty-five years ago, except for the lack of ocean. It's still underdeveloped, people are friendly, traffic doesn't exist, and the trees outnumber the buildings. Main Street is right out of a Norman Rockwell painting, with one-of-a-kind shops and one good restaurant. The downside of this is most of the other restaurants are chains. The best store is TJ Maxx, though not a problem for me. The only movie theater is showing *Jurassic Park*, and the nearest bagel shop is in Daytona Beach. And I am freezing! And thankfully, the weekend is almost over. We will visit our friends again in warmer weather.

For the moment, I've had my fill of small towns, Spanish moss, and manatee watching, and I'm actually looking forward to going home . . . to the chaos, the crowds, and the comforts of home on the bay.

I guess I learned my lesson. The "getaway" got me to appreciate what I've already got.

Love to you all.

Alexa
Aka Trailer Trash

*A typical male, T-Rex refused to read the instructions before taking the second dose of cough syrup without eating. The codeine in it made him sick to his stomach. It's not pretty when a T-Rex throws up. Can I please go home now?

June 21, 2016
Roan Mountain, North Carolina
"Think Pink"

How to begin? It started earlier in the day with a ride up to Roan Mountain, NC, for the annual Rhododendron Festival. The "rhodo" is a fuchsia pink, five-pointed star (not six points around here) flower. Every third week in June, for seventy years, hikers and blossom lovers have flocked to the mountaintop to view the pink profusion. "Think pink" is repeated on every road sign, T-shirt, and shop window. The mountain, normally a lush green, white with snow or black on a moonless night, turns pink, hot pink, and cherries-in-the-snow pink, and this year, the festival weekend hit the peak of pink. Definitely worth the drive!

Just down the mountain, the little town of Bakersville hosts the festival. On the grounds, we found the usual health food choices of funnel cakes, sweet tea, and barbeque, accompanied by a fiddlin' and rockabilly band on a stage near the creek.

But there was talk in the crowds of something else—something going on later, that night at the school. Whispers of "Wonder who it will be?" and "Be sure to git there early" were everywhere. Since bashfulness is not a trait of T-Rex or myself, we asked one of the locals what *it* was going to be. "Why, it's the pageant. Tonight, they crown the new rhododendron queen." T-Rex rolled his eyes at the thought, but mine lit up, and I knew I just had to go. He agreed only after there was some bargaining. Yes, he could watch the Military Channel later, and I'm not allowed to tell any of his friends he went to a beauty pageant, and if it was really awful, we would leave. Deal! (Two out of three ain't bad.)

We drove to Bowman Middle School. The pageant was to be held in the auditorium at 7:00 p.m. We arrived to find crowds of pageant-goers and an almost full parking lot. But unlike Miami, there were no policemen or horns honking.

We were asked to pay $10.00 each at the door. Candies, popcorn, sodas, and water were for sale for a dollar. We found two seats close to the stage and the giant T runway, which was decorated with pink plastic flowers and twinkle lights. It wasn't the Fontainebleau, but it was pretty in a tacky sort of way. T-Rex was already squirming, but I settled in with skeptical anticipation and tried to ignore him. The lights dimmed, and a well-spoken Southern gentleman, who reminded me of Dick VanDyke with a Southern accent, appeared in a tuxedo with a pink flower in his lapel. He was the MC. This was starting to look less amateurish. T-Rex was still squirming.

The music began, and a parade of previous rhodo queens began, some from the '60s, '70s, '80s, and '90s. They all were wearing black and pink. Oh my God. Is there no end to the pink thing? But they looked lovely, and according to their bios, were accomplished women—the kind who could've stepped out of the pages of *Good Housekeeping*, *Look Magazine*, or a Breck shampoo commercial. In addition, queens from other counties were introduced, and we met the watermelon queen, the dogwood queen, the thresher queen, and the strawberry festival queen. They were all in gowns and tiaras. Cheesy? Yes. Small town? Yes! But this is a big deal around these counties and one that has been given great thought and planning. My big-city skepticism was turning into admiration. T-Rex was sitting up straighter and keeping still.

The current finalists had been judged on their interviews and swimsuits the previous night. Tonight would be talent and evening gowns. And so it began, one by one, as the eighteen- and nineteen-year-olds sang, acted out monologues, and tap-danced. There were no baton twirlers. I started to weed out (no pun intended) my top picks, and T-Rex did, too. The lady sitting next to him was the grandmother of one of the contestants and filled him in on some of the other families. Squirming was at a dead halt as he listened like a polite schoolboy.

After intermission, the queen from 1996 came on stage and belted out a Trisha Yearwood song called "Don't Put Me in the Corner." She was so good, we wished she would have sung more. Turns out, after her year as queen, she went on to become the lead singer in a band that travels the southeast.

How times have changed. I remember watching the Miss America contest as a little girl with my best friend Marci. We both wanted to be her someday. Only problem was, neither of us had the required bust and hip measurements, and we sure didn't have a talent. We also wanted to be flight attendants, which seemed more realistic back then. But if I wanted to become Miss America today, I would aspire to be almost anything: a brain surgeon, an author, a rock star, and yes, the president of the United States. And I have no doubt that even in the little rural town of Bakersville, some of these girls will have great futures. And even if they don't, they will have tonight and these moments.

The lights dimmed again, and the evening gown competition began. Some walked less gracefully on the runway, probably due to the unfamiliarity of high heels or nervous knees shaking. I was amazed at the gowns. I guess I was expecting homemade, unsophisticated dresses, but oh no . . . With the exception of one, they were all store-bought, some with crisscrossed back straps, illusion netting, halter necklines, bejeweled skirts, and little cleavage. We are in the Bible Belt, and the opening prayer and constant references to the Father and his son are meant to be reminders of modesty.

I selected my favorite gown, worn on a girl with the right measurements. It was the color of the inside of a conch shell, the palest pink blush, dotted with rhinestones. She conjured up the image of a cotton candy princess, demure and delicious to see.

The four judges deliberated for at least twenty minutes, and the tension in the auditorium was silently palpable. T-Rex and I had narrowed our choices down to two. The winner would receive a $5,000 scholarship and travel the counties doing queen things for the next year. Finally, the MC came back to the podium, and he announced the winners. Amid the usual tears and shrieks, Miss Congeniality, the runners-up, and then the winner came forth. I had picked the winner for the gown,

Miss Cotton Candy, but not the new 2016 rhododendron queen who had bowled us over with her jazz tap dance to Michael Jackson's "Thriller." Apparently, she had also earned high marks the night before. But no problem. At that point, they all seemed like winners to me.

As an adult, I do think it's a bit ridiculous to see women parading around in high heels and swimsuits, even though that's considered a fashion statement on South Beach. However, after sitting through this pageant, I realized that this is an opportunity for these girls, a real step up toward their futures. As for T-Rex, I wish I had had a video recording of him smiling and applauding, and yes, standing up for the winners. He thought tonight was special, and he acknowledged that the Military Channel will wait. Skepticism and squirming are in the past. Tomorrow, I'll be wearing pink and will be thinking pink for a long time.

There she, is Miss Rhododendron, the possible future president of the United States, or maybe the best damn manicurist in western North Carolina.

Love to you all.

Alexa
Aka Trailer Trash

2017

June 18, 2017
So, You Think You Can Go RVing?

We think we can, so here we go again. We are older and maybe wiser, and I find it is easier to go RVing now. Why? Because I've made my mantra on the road, "So what!" As in, so what if I forgot my toothbrush or the power cord to my laptop? (Which I did.) After all, the USA is not exactly a wilderness.

It's day one, and T-Rex rolled us out before dawn, barking orders like a general. But I know the drill and just smile. We are heading for Destin, FL, and then onward to Roswell, New Mexico, for the annual UFO convention. There will be some strange and wonderful characters out there. Could it be more like a family reunion for T-Rex?

Day one is now in competition for "the longest day," which I wrote about ten years ago. I hate to complain so early in the adventure, but damn, eleven hours in the truck tested my ability to occupy myself and remain cheerful. Florida must be the longest state in the United States, and we almost covered it in 625 miles. T-Rex drove all the way in good humor and never seemed to tire, which further annoyed me. How *does* he do it?

It's an hour earlier in Destin. That's really great. The longest day just got longer. Sounds familiar.

We settled in at Camp Gulf, one of the only RV parks right on the beach. How ironic that living on Miami Beach, it never occurs to me to go to the beach. Here, we could hardly wait. The next morning at 8:30 a.m., and in less than five minutes from our site, we were walking on sugar-white sand as fine as Pillsbury's best flour. Sugar, flour, and yes, there is baking, but the bronzed and burnt bodies heading for their place in the sun do not look good enough to eat. Don't they hear me repeating "SPF, SPF" under my hat and sunblock?

But, what a dazzling sight to see the Gulf waters and the line of trailers dotting the beachside. Plus, it's Father's Day. There are lots of families, strollers, beach chairs, umbrellas, and beer. Remember, it's "not just for breakfast anymore."

There has been talk of going swimming, which means the dreaded experience of shopping for a bathing suit (I purposely did not bring one again). This normally involves the added humiliation of a three-way mirror. Maybe it'll rain.

Love to you all.

Alexa
Aka Trailer Trash

June 19, 2017
Pastels, Pickets (Fences), and Porches

What a surprise! Just fifteen minutes from Destin are the incredibly picturesque, planned communities of Seaside and Watercolor. Soft pastels set the old Florida mood on every home and all the restaurants and shops.

Seaside is the first city in America designed on the principles of "urbanism." This upscale beach town is the brainchild of architects Andrés Duany and Elizabeth Plater-Zybek. The homes are in the Southern vernacular style with wraparound porches, metal roofs, and picket fences, but no front yards, only native plants, and no sod.

There is a town square, real bookstores, and one-of-a-kind boutiques. There are no chain stores of any kind, and all the parking (if you can find a space) is free.

Right next door, there's another planned community—the town of Watercolor, aptly named. In addition to the pale pinks and greens, it has a beautiful inn that reminds me of a Ralph Lauren ad—crisp white with navy- and sky-blue accents, and great-looking, tanned, fit guests.

It's crowded in these towns, and everyone, I mean everyone,

is riding bicycles. That sure helps with traffic and parking. This area of the Florida Panhandle used to be called the "Redneck Riviera," but that has all changed. Along with the seafoam greens, lemon yellows, and conch shell pinks, I saw the color of money everywhere. How about a root beer float for $7.50, or a bathing suit for $330.00? Real estate prices here make Miami look like a bargain.

However, at Bud and Alley's Restaurant, we did have the best crabcakes I have ever eaten and the second-best key lime pie, along with a spectacular view of the Gulf. Trailer Trash could get used to this.

A couple of things to note: The movie, *The Truman Show*, with Jim Carrey, was filmed here, and all the public bathrooms are air-conditioned.

Driving back to Destin, I felt like I had spent my entire day inside a beautiful painting.

Love to you all.

Alexa
Aka Trailer Trash

(I dodged the bathing suit bullet again.)

June 22, 2017
Old Man River

Tropical Storm Cindy washed out our New Orleans sightseeing to almost zero. However, during a break in the storm, we took the big truck and drove to one of the levees near the RV park. The wind was so strong that I needed an anchor, and T-Rex fit the bill. Arms locked together, we climbed up to the top of the levee and looked out at the "Mighty Mississippi." It's an intimidating sight. Today, it's grey and churning but not at a threatening level. It's vast and not hard to imagine that the water could overcome some of the twenty-one-foot levees around the city.

Did you know that sixty percent of all grain exported from the United States is shipped on the Mississippi through the port of New Orleans and the port of south Louisiana? And did you know that the river contains at least 250 species of fish, 145 species of amphibians and reptiles (yikes), and that sixty percent of all North American birds use the river basin as their migrating flyaway?

On the river right in front of us were huge freighter ships lined up, waiting their turn to enter the port, and even larger barges being pushed by mega tugboats. Just as I was thinking about the Broadway musical *Showboat* and life on the river, along the top of the levee came a woman jogging against the wind. I said hello and asked her questions about the levees, and boy, did she have answers and her own story.

She was a victim of Hurricane Katrina, rescued after three days on a rooftop by a helicopter. She was eleven years old at the time, displaced to Texas, and separated from her family for three months with no communication. A nice family took her in and made sure she went to school. Now, with a family of her own, she still becomes traumatized when she hears the words "storm warning." I sympathized and thanked her for telling me her story, during which her eyes became teary and spilled over. We exchanged names. Hers is Brianna.

Although most people visiting New Orleans go to the French Quarter, eat in fabulous restaurants, and listen to great music in sleazy bars, weather was not permitting. Maybe next time. But for this time, I'll never forget people like Brianna and the river. In spite of all their ups and downs, they keep on rolling.

Love to you all.

Alexa
Aka Trailer Trash

July 1, 2017
Deer Catchers and Koozies

If you live in south central or mid-Texas, these are the must-have essentials: a truck, a deer catcher on the front of your truck, a koozie, cowboy boots, and a gun. For the unenlightened, including me, a Texas koozie is a leather wrap that goes around your beer to keep it cold. Most of them are laced up on one side and start out being a light brown color and then darken with use. The deer catchers may be self-explanatory, but just in case, picture a thick metal grill mounted across a truck's front bumper. The deer are everywhere out here, and they can cause a lot of damage to a vehicle.

How did a city girl princess find out all of this? Well, when we were in Luckenbach, Texas, I spotted a very interesting-looking woman at the outside bar. It was midday, and she was drinking a beer wrapped in a koozie, and she was wearing a great-looking cowboy hat. Luckenbach has a population of three, so I wondered where she fit in to the community. Turns out Selena was happy to talk to me, and when I asked her about herself, she quoted the slogan of the town: "Everybody's somebody in Luckenbach," which is also the title of a honky-tonk song by Dale Watson.

Selena had made her cowboy hat band out of wine and beer bottle tops and had a turquoise ring on every unmanicured finger. She wasn't young, but she looked tough and fit, and I could imagine her barrel-racing on a horse. She explained all about the koozie, and I'm sure hers, which had turned very dark brown, had been wrapped around many a beer. Her face was lined like old leather, but she had a great smile and perfect teeth.

Luckenbach, Texas, was the inspiration for a great Willie Nelson and Waylon Jennings song, and they used to put on concerts in the town that attracted thousands. Selena's mother was the appointed sheriff of the town back then, but now Luckenbach is more of a business than a community. Selena told me that her sons think she's "different," and I guess she is by anyone's standards.

I asked where she lived, and she said, "Way out in the country."

"Aren't you afraid out there all alone?" I asked.

Her answer was classic Texas. "Nope. I've got five reasons not to be scared." She proceeded to describe all of her guns, shotguns, etc.

FYI, Texas passed an open-carry law in 2016 that allows concealed handgun permit holders to carry handguns openly. T-Rex, a major gun enthusiast, was doing his happy dance the entire time we were in Texas.

Selena also told me that even with a deer catcher on her truck, a big spotted deer hit her truck and smashed her headlights.

If you are so inclined, go to YouTube and put in "Luckenbach Texas." It's a great song about getting back to the basics, and would you believe that two New Yorkers who had never been to Texas wrote it?

We're leaving the beautiful green hill country of Texas tomorrow and heading for Roswell, New Mexico. The desert.

Love to you all.

Alexa
Aka Trailer Trash

June 26, 2017
Meanwhile, Back at the Ranch . . .

Today we had a rendezvous with the land on the LBJ Ranch. Politics aside, Lyndon B. Johnson was a president like no other. He was born in a farmhouse to a poor family, walked four miles to a one-room schoolhouse, eventually taught school, and rose through the ranks of the Democratic party. The good news includes his domestic policies. He led the first civil rights bill to prevent segregation and ensure voting rights for all, and called for the peaceful exploration of outer space. His "Great Society" put the emphasis on health and education (Head Start), pollution, and the preservation of natural resources. In 1965, he signed Medicare into law but gave credit to Truman for "starting it all." Luckily, for all of us, in 1972, his family donated 2,000 acres of the 3,000-acre LBJ Ranch to Texas Parks and Wildlife, and it is now a historic state park. What a difference a presidency makes . . . if you know what I mean. The bad news is, he was crude, domineering, married for money, womanized, and escalated our involvement in the Vietnam War. What a difference a presidency makes. Now you know what I mean.

The ranch is a beautiful contrast to his big bold personality. It is big—3,000 acres—but it's a place of serenity in the rolling hill country in Stonewall, TX. It's isolated, genteel, and quiet. Heads of state from all over the world met there, and they must have wondered at the modest home, the prized Herefords, and working ranch. We were able to see the bedrooms, bathrooms, closets, kitchen, living room, airstrip, and the cemetery. It was a time before cell phones, and there were dial telephones in every room. Do you remember the TV sets with small screens and large consoles? These were always set to the news stations.

His wife, Lady Bird, was well educated and wealthy. She bankrolled LBJ's congressional campaign, bought a radio station, and then a TV station, which made them millionaires. She was an avid reader, and we were told that the only TV show she ever watched was "Gunsmoke" on Saturday night. Her favorite color was yellow, and good taste was not one of her strong points, but her love and appreciation of nature brought us the Highway Beautification Act. She and actress Helen Hayes also founded the National Wildflower Research Center west of Austin. When LBJ died of a heart attack, the couple's eldest daughter, Lynda, said, "God knew what he was doing when Daddy died ahead of Mother." She thought her father would not have been able to live without Lady Bird. So, in spite of his womanizing, apparently LBJ loved her and depended on her support and strength of character. She died thirty-four years after LBJ at the age of ninety-four.

Now that I've bored you with the historical facts that you probably knew but had forgotten, I must tell you about the land. T-Rex and I drove the tour paths in the truck and fell in love with the place. It's still a working ranch and designated open range, which means the cows meander without fences, in front or alongside your truck, on any and every pathway. Agile spotted deer are everywhere, jumping the hillsides with their fragile babies running behind them. Horses are grazing, and birds in flight dip and soar in the breezes. It's truly a respite from the world.

We got out of the truck at the family cemetery and sat for a long time under the 500-year-old oak trees. This ranch was the Johnsons' "heart home," and after a while, we could understand the peacefulness that it must have brought to the president. It was said he spent twenty-five percent of his presidency at the "Texas White House." Lady Bird called it "a place worth holding together." President Kennedy only visited the ranch once. He was scheduled to make his second visit after his stop in Dallas. And the rest is the unfortunate history.

So long for now. I'll be back in touch soon.

Love to you all.

Alexa
Aka Trailer Trash

July 2, 2017
Roswell, New Mexico
"The Truth Is Out There . . ." Maybe.

Everyone has their own "truth." To know this, all you have to do is watch fake news. In this case, however, I'm talking about UFOs and aliens and the people who believe they exist. We deliberately traveled to Roswell, NM, for the annual UFO convention. It's the 70th anniversary of the world-famous UFO crash. Just as a reminder, in 1947, a US Air Force balloon (others believe the object was extraterrestrial) crashed on a farmer's ranch in Corona, NM. For some reason, Roswell got the credit for the landing, and the rest is sci-fi history. This is a three-day gathering of "believers" who dress up, give lectures, and basically revel in anything sci-fi. We were not disappointed. As we entered our RV park, the first thing we saw was a giant green cardboard alien sign welcoming us, and things got greener and more alien as the days progressed.

Downtown Roswell isn't much. There's one main street, and the streetlights are all in the shape of alien heads. Kinda cool when they're lit. Kinda creepy if you're not into aliens. Every store window has some kind of display reminding us that we've "come to shop," and there are hundreds of tacky souvenirs. At the UFO Museum, we saw videos of the supposed UFO crash landing in 1947 and the captured alien. There is a lifelike exhibit of an alien autopsy and a video of aliens landing with their spaceship. The place was mobbed with tourists. I haven't read any, but there are a lot of books written about "close encounters," and many of those authors were there to sign books and give lectures. There are panel discussions, and participants tell of their abductions and sightings. And you thought you had weird friends!

Out on the streets, it was 107 degrees, and to cool off, we dashed under misting stations—like the vegetable bins in a Publix grocery store. Main Street is where the real show happens. Every kind of person, child, and dog is dressed up for the occasion. Kitschy creativity rules, and there's more aluminum foil worn than Reynolds has in stock. As if it were completely normal, people were walking around with futuristic headgear, shaved painted heads, colored plastic goggles, wings, tails, antennas, artificial body parts, exposed body parts, green tights, pink bodysuits, ray guns, and so on and so on. T-Rex was primed for the humanoid costume contest the next day.

But first, we had to go to the doggie costume party in the park. It was early in the morning, so the temperature was in the bearable 80s and made more bearable by the cute canines on parade. Try to picture multiple chihuahuas on board a spaceship made from a silver umbrella, or a giant Great Dane wearing goggles and painted green with peace signs, or a Jack Russell terrier with spider legs made from felt attached to a vest. As funny as the dogs were, the owners were over the top.

They too were decked out in sci-fi's finest garb. The Great Dane won, I think because he looked so forlorn. Or maybe size does count.

In between all the madness, we went to my first laser light show. It was in Roswell's Goddard Planetarium. We had selected the show accompanied by country music, and I was enthralled with the rapid-fire digital visuals telling the stories of cowboys, trucks, mama, lost love, and whiskey. There were no comets or quasars, but the night sky was filled with musical stars. I loved it.

Today was the humanoid costume party. T-Rex wanted to get there early for a good seat. The place was packed, and we sat in the second row. The moderator was someone named Josh Gates from the Travel Channel. He's doing a TV special called "Expedition Unknown: Hunt for Extraterrestrials," so this was a perfect place for him. And then, one by one, the contestants came to the front of the stage. Every age, size, and shape appeared. We gasped, giggled, covered our eyes—well, T-Rex didn't—and applauded. This was a spectacle of creativity, garishness, immodesty, beauty, and over-the-top fun. The standouts included a sister and brother encased in colorful balloons. I named them the bubble children. Another "standout," literally, was a man in a skintight hot-pink bodysuit, leaving nothing to the imagination, and a puppet-wielding gigantic woman in a more gigantic plastic green suit. She was a ventriloquist, whispering sweet alien nothings in her puppet's ears. My favorite was a woman carrying multiple black umbrellas that were lit up with blinking lights from underneath. Dressed in all black, she appeared as the antithesis to the black hole—sparkling and twinkling.

The winner was a graceful young woman in ballet shoes who had danced around the stage. Not my choice, but maybe she was a droid?

That night was the parade, but all the streetlights suddenly went out, and we really didn't see much. Not sure what happened . . . Maybe the extraterrestrials were tired of being imitated, or maybe it was the local electrical storm that shut down the power for several blocks. Another mystery to ponder.

The other close encounter we had was with a group called Steam Punkers. I had never heard of them, and they were a strange-looking lot. Steampunk is a universal sub-genre of science fiction that combines historical elements from the industrial age with current technology. Basically, it's combining the old with the new, with a strong Victorian bent. They are "an homage to vintage, with a modern, sassy twist." This homage is evident in their beliefs, their dress, their books, and their music. It's a colorful protest against the inevitable advance of technology. My curiosity helped me overcome my fear of this weirdness. I had to talk to some of them, and even though some carried swords and wore lizard heads, they were friendly. They make things by hand—beautiful, useful items made out of leather, brass, and copper, harkening back to tinkers, tailors, and candlestick makers. They dress as pirates, villains, and explorers, and they're time travelers with conventions all over the world.

I do understand the ideas of a movement back to a time when there were rules to be followed, and greater civility, plus glamour and mystery. Who among us wouldn't enjoy rescuing a damsel in distress or being carried off by a handsome man in a red velvet cloak?

And so, the mystery of the "Roswell incident" continues. It's certainly become a business boon for the town. What do I think? I think I'd like to believe. I think that with so much out in space, why should we be the only ones with life on our planet? And I think that if intelligent life has come to this planet, it's not a moment too soon.

In the meantime, I'll be looking for the man in the red velvet cloak. T-Rex, are you listening?

Love to you all.

Alexa
Aka Trailer Trash

What a difference it made when I took the road less traveled.

I'm so glad I did.

Acknowledgments

My tiara is off to:

Jeremy, my perfect son, and Carolyn, my perfect daughter-in-law, who showered me with encouragement and technical support.
Helen Ellis, author extraordinaire, who told me to "keep writing."
Margie Klein, friend and author, who guided me.
My grammatically-correct mother.
My father, who loved the wide-open spaces.
All the trashette friends who wanted more stories.
Jesse at A Darned Good Book.
Noah Valentine Styles, the book-cover maven.
Editing Wizard, Sarah Flores, at Write Down The Line, L.L.C.

About the Author

Alexa Rossy has been writing poems, limericks, short stories, and letters to the editor for years. She decided it was time to turn her passion for traveling, and talking to strangers into stories that might inspire others to create their own experiences.

Alexa was born and raised in glamourous Miami Beach but has traveled extensively. Her summers were usually spent in the Blue Ridge Mountains, where she rode quarter horses and learned to appreciate the simple pleasures of rural life.

She has degrees from the University of Miami and Boston University School of Journalism. She has worked as a public relations copywriter, a descriptive writer for architects and a personal ghostwriter for many.

When she's not RVing, Alexa is at home in Miami trying to memorize her passwords and polishing the good silver.

Contact her at TrailerTrashette@gmail.com

Made in United States
Orlando, FL
21 November 2023